BIDDY MASON SPEAKS UP

by Arisa White and Laura Atkins

Illustrations by Laura Freeman

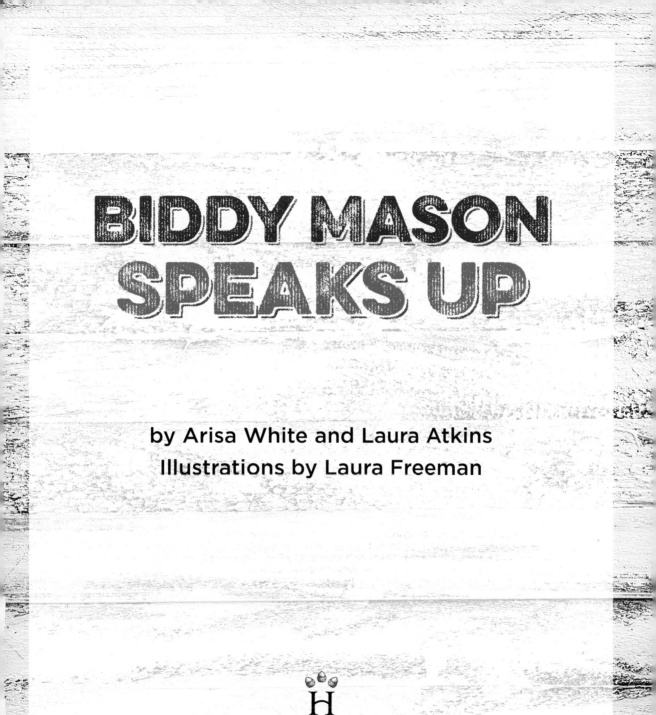

Heyday, Berkeley, California

WHAT IS HISTORY, AND WHY DO WE TELL STORIES?

The record we call "history" does not tell everyone's story.

We faced this challenge when we decided to write about Biddy Mason. She was held captive and enslaved along with millions of Black people in our country. People in power did not allow her, or most enslaved people, to learn to read or write. Enslaved peoples' stories were rarely recorded or valued by the White people who kept records—the records that became our nation's "history."

Writing this book was a creative act of repairing the historical record, of imagining Biddy Mason's life based on all the information and stories we could gather. We believe that we are all better when we hear everyone's stories, especially those that have been silenced.

This is not the story of a single person doing a single heroic act. It is the story of collective effort. Biddy used plants and healing to fulfill her dreams of freedom and home ownership with the support of women helping women, free Black people helping enslaved Black people, and a network that extended across states and races.

Now more than ever, we need to understand that we do not do anything alone. We are interconnected. As Biddy Mason said, "Nothing good can come into a closed hand."

Text © 2019 by Arisa White and Laura Atkins
Illustrations © 2019 by Laura Freeman

Library of Congress Cataloging-in-Publication Data

Names: White, Arisa, author. | Atkins, Laura, author. | Freeman, Laura
  (Illustrator), illustrator.
Title: Biddy Mason speaks up / by Arisa White and Laura Atkins ;
  illustrations by Laura Freeman.
Description: Berkeley, California : Heyday, [2019] | Includes bibliographical
  references and index.
Identifiers: LCCN 2018010807 | ISBN 9781597144032 (hardcover : alk. paper)
Subjects: LCSH: Mason, Biddy, 1818-1891--Juvenile literature. | Women
  slaves--United States--Biography--Juvenile literature. | Slaves--United
  States--Biography--Juvenile literature. | African American
  women--Biography--Juvenile literature. | African American
  midwives--California--Biography--Juvenile literature. | Overland journeys
  to the Pacific--Juvenile literature. | African American
  women--California--Biography--Juvenile literature. |
  Freedmen--California--Biography--Juvenile literature. | Frontier and
  pioneer life--California--Juvenile literature.
Classification: LCC E444.M38 W47 2019 | DDC 306.3/62092 [B]--dc23
LC record available at https://lccn.loc.gov/2018010807

Cover Illustration: Laura Freeman
Back Cover Photographs (from left to right): by Dorothea Lange, courtesy of
the National Archives and Records Administration; courtesy of Charles E. Young
Research Library, UCLA; courtesy of UCLA Library Special Collections
Interior Design/Typesetting: Nancy Austin Design
See Image Credits and Permissions on page 97

Orders, inquiries, and correspondence should be addressed to:
  Heyday
  P.O. Box 9145, Berkeley, CA 94709
  (510) 549-3564, Fax (510) 549-1889
  www.heydaybooks.com

Printed in China by Regent Publishing Services, Hong Kong

10 9 8 7 6 5 4 3 2 1

CONTENTS

1.
HEALING

On a cool Sunday morning,
seven-year-old Biddy
and Granny Ellen
tread carefully
through the woods.

"See those oval-shaped
leaves?" Granny points.
Biddy rubs the slippery
leaves through her fingers.
"We use plantain to make
a salve for cuts and slashes
we get from work in the fields,"
Granny says.

She has taken care
of Biddy since she was sold
away from her mother
as a baby.
Even though Granny
isn't allowed to read
or write, she knows
how to read plants.

"Nature is like an open hand.
It gives in abundance,"
Granny explains.

She shows Biddy
fuzzy white clusters of boneset
that bring down a fever,
and snakeroot's purple
flowers that heal snakebites.

"We must be like nature,"
Granny Ellen says,
"because nothing good can
come when we close
our hands to others."

Granny takes
Biddy's hand.
As they tread on,
she sings:
"I sought my Lord in the wilderness,
for I'm a-going home...."

Biddy feels free
in the woods.
She thinks,
*I want to be
a healer like Granny
and help my
pulled-together
family survive.*

Biddy picks peach leaves
to make a tea that will
rid Uncle Eugene of

stomach worms he got
from poorly cooked pork
Master gives them to eat.

Back at their place,
Biddy mashes up
greenbrier leaves
with hog lard to make
a salve for ten-year-old
Lula's burn.

Mistress overheard
Lula say she was tired
from tending to the baby
for twelve hours straight.
Mistress ran a hot iron
down Lula's arm
"to teach her some respect."
The salve will return
Lula's skin to brown.

Out of breath,
Aunt Della's husband
hollers into the door,
"She's starting to labor!"

Biddy packs Granny's
bag with clean clothes,
string, oils, teas, and
a clean sharp knife.
The gift for the baby,
a doll she made
from an old flour sack,
goes into her pocket.

Tea made from peach leaves gets rid
of intestinal worms.

PEACH

Quickly they head
to Della's quarters.
Biddy starts a fire
to boil water. She
then puts an ax
under Della's bed.

Biddy learned
from Granny Ellen
who learned from
her own granny
in Africa that
"the ax cuts the pain."

Biddy knows
when it's time
to position her
body behind
Della's lower back
to take the pressure off.

Della's moans
become deep and loud.
Together,
Granny and Biddy say,
"Push, Della, push."

Boneset brings down a fever.

BONESET

SLAVERY AND MIDWIFERY

Bridget "Biddy" Mason was born in Hancock County, Georgia, in 1818, where she was enslaved. The law prevented enslaved people from learning to read or write, so it was difficult for people like Biddy to record their own experiences in this way. We know very little about her early years, and had to imagine this time in Biddy's life using historical research, "slave narratives" (written accounts by enslaved people after escaping slavery), and audio interviews with people who lived during the same period and in similar regions.

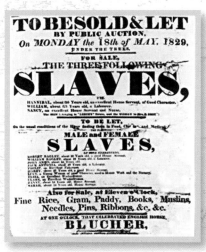

Slavery is the brutal practice of human beings owning other human beings. In the United States, people of European ancestry in positions of power decided that they could make more money if other people worked for them for free. In what is known as the Trans-Atlantic Slave Trade, African people were captured and kidnapped from their homes and families, taken on ships across the ocean to the United States, and sold to slave owners who forced them to work for no pay. Slavery operated legally in the United States for hundreds of years.

ENSLAVED: when someone is held as a slave and loses their freedom of choice and action. Many people prefer the term "enslaved person" instead of "slave." "Slave" is a noun that defines a person only according to the system of slavery. "Enslaved" is an adjective that speaks to how that person was treated.

LAW: a rule that the government makes.

LEGAL: permitted by, or follows, the law.

RIGHT: a freedom that people have to be, do, or have something.

The United States Constitution, first written in 1789, outlines the system of beliefs and laws that were designed to govern the country. The Constitution declares that "all men are created equal." But enslaved people were not given equal rights. In fact, the Constitution protected slavery, and twelve of our nation's first presidents were enslavers.

Power Discussed

Power can mean many things, and can exist and work in many ways. A basic definition of power is the ability to produce an effect. It can also mean control or influence over others. How do you see power at work in your community, and in our country?

INSTITUTIONAL POWER

COLLECTIVE POWER

PERSONAL POWER

EMPOWERMENT

People developed the concept of race in part to defend slavery in the United States. This idea of race and racial difference depended on White supremacy and racism. European Americans in positions of power called themselves "White" in order to set themselves apart from the people they called "Black" and "Mulatto." European Americans saw people of African ancestry as being less human. To this day, people of African ancestry continue to face racism in our country. While we use the terms White and Black (or African American) in this book, we do so knowing that these terms are not based on biology. Race is a made-up concept, but because of how institutions and society treat people, race continues to deeply shape and impact people's lives.

This picture shows several generations of an enslaved family in South Carolina in 1862. While we invented the character of Granny Ellen for this book, we know that Biddy had tight relationships with those around her. Enslaved African Americans could not control where their families or friends went and were constantly having people they loved taken away from them. As a result, they deeply valued community and created families based on who was around them.

Enslaved women who became midwives empowered Black people to have some control over their own bodies by making choices about their health. That feeling of personal power was important to healing. Knowledge of plant medicine and birth practices were passed down from generation to generation. "Granny" was often the title given to older enslaved women and to midwives as a show of respect for their age and wisdom.

MIDWIFE: typically a woman who is trained to help females in childbirth, and who has a knowledge of herbal remedies and healthcare. A midwife tends to the spirit as well as to the body.

"Old Sibby Kelly" was a midwife who was said to have delivered more babies than any White doctor in Glynn County, Georgia. Biddy would have learned midwifery from such a woman.

Though it was illegal for enslaved people to marry, they held "jumping the broom" ceremonies in their communities as a way to celebrate and honor partnerships. Loving relationships and community connections helped people face the extreme hardships of slavery.

THE BROOMSTICK WEDDING.

TIMELINE

1500s–1808
The United States is part of the Trans-Atlantic Slave Trade.

1776
The United States becomes an independent nation from England.

1807
The Act Prohibiting Importation of Slaves is passed, stopping new enslaved people from being legally brought into the United States.

1818
August 15
Biddy Mason is born in Hancock County, Georgia.

1820
The US Census states the total population to be 9,638,453, with 1,538,022 enslaved.

2.
PLANTATION WOUNDS

Monday morning
and the sun's not yet up.
Biddy and Granny Ellen are
already picking cotton.

Now in her teens,
Biddy shoves fistfuls
of cotton into the burlap bag
strapped across her chest.

Heavy on
Biddy's shoulders
is the August heat.
Down one row, up another.
Back and forth
until the last sun ray.
They must pick
150 pounds each day.

The overseer
puts Granny's bags
on the scale.
The lines on
his forehead show
it's not enough.

He raises his rawhide
whip high in the air,
and brings it down
on Granny Ellen.

Each time the whip
strikes, Biddy winces.
Again and again
like her own
body is being hit.

She wants to throw
herself over Granny's back—
but stops herself.
*What good will
I be to Granny
if I'm whipped?*

Granny is carried
to their quarters.
As Biddy mixes
the plantain salve
to apply to Granny's
welts and broken skin,
Biddy's tears fall in.

The next morning,
beneath a red-hot sun,
Biddy watches Granny's
bent-over back,
the slow way her fingers
pick cotton, the silver
streaks in her hair.
Biddy quickens her pace.

PLANTAIN

Plantain can be made into a salve to treat skin injuries and reduce swelling.

PLANTATION LIFE AND PICKING COTTON

Biddy probably grew up on a cotton plantation. Cotton, a major cash crop, was grown throughout the Cotton Belt states. Plantation owners usually kept many enslaved people to plant and harvest their cotton, and also to serve the slave owner's family.

PLANTATION: a large-scale farm that grows cash crops like cotton, rice, sugar, and tobacco.

CASH CROP: a crop that is grown to be sold, instead of being used by the people who grow it.

COTTON BELT: in the mid-1800s, the region of the Southern United States that produced the most cotton.

MASTER/MISTRESS: a man or woman who owns enslaved people.

DRIVER: a person who makes sure enslaved people do their work, and who can carry out harsh physical abuse.

The master, mistress, and their children usually lived in what was called the "big house," while the people they enslaved lived in small quarters nearby, sometimes called "slave row." Houses for enslaved people were very basic, often with dirt floors, beds of straw (if there were beds at all), and cracks in the walls that let in the cold, heat, and rain.

"Field slaves" on a cotton plantation spent six or more days each week working in the fields. They cleared land, and planted, tended, and harvested cotton from sunrise until after sunset, as this photo from 1850 shows. The driver watched them closely to make sure no one stopped working and would use abuse such as whipping or denying water. "It was rarely that a day passed by without one or more whippings," Solomon Northup wrote in the book *Twelve Years a Slave.* "[T]he crack of the lash and the shrieking of the slaves can be heard from dark till bedtime."

Slave Codes

WHAT ARE THE BARRIERS THAT KEEP YOU FROM SPEAKING UP?

Slave codes were state laws that controlled and defined enslaved people as property, rather than as human beings. White lawmakers created these laws to prevent enslaved people from rebelling or escaping, and in order to have complete control over Black bodies. Here are a few examples:

- Enslaved people could not legally marry.
- In Mississippi, the penalty for teaching an enslaved person to read or educating them about their circumstances was imprisonment or death.
- In Georgia, "Any person who sees more than seven men slaves without any White person, in a high road, may whip each slave twenty lashes."

PROPERTY: a thing, or things, that belong to someone; something that is owned.

Most children started working in the fields between the ages of eight and twelve, but all children helped with chores. Mary Island of Louisiana recalled "[w]ashing dishes when I was four years old and when I was six... I carried water.... When I got to be seven years old, I was cutting sprouts almost like a man, and when I was eight, I could pick one hundred pounds of cotton."

Mingo White of Alabama said, "I weren't nothing but a child, but I had to work the same as any man. I went into the field and hoed cotton, pulled fodder, and picked cotton with the rest of the hands.... In the winter I went to the woods with the menfolks to help get wood."

TIMELINE

1800–1860
In 1800, the United States produced 156,000 bales of cotton, which by 1860 increased to 4 millions bales. One bale of cotton weighs 400 to 500 pounds.

1830
The US Census records the population of the 24 states of the U.S. to be 12,866,020, with 2,009,043 enslaved.

1850s
Around 75 percent of enslaved people in the United States work in the cotton industry.

3.
STOLEN AND CARRIED AWAY

It is like someone dies
when Biddy and her two daughters
are taken from Granny Ellen
and the only family
she's known.

Granny's wails follow Biddy
to the household of Robert
and Rebecca Dorn Smith.
Biddy, now twenty-five years old,
and her daughters,
six-year-old Ellen
and one-year-old Ann,
have become the Smiths' property.

Biddy never sees Granny Ellen again.
But every time she calls
her oldest daughter's name,
Granny is remembered.

In the Smiths' small house,
they sleep on the kitchen floor,
keeping warm with the quilt
Aunt Della made
from rags and scraps of cloth
so Biddy won't forget their love.

Their days are marked
by the tick-tock of the
Smiths' grandfather clock.
Before sunrise, Biddy
and her girls wake
to chop wood, fetch water,
make breakfast for the Smiths.
Some days, Biddy picks sassafras to brew a tonic
for the sick mistress, and then
continues on with her daily chores.

Not too long
after they arrive,
Master forces his way
onto Biddy while she's
harvesting sweet corn
in the field.

He covers her mouth
and threatens to sell her
away from her daughters
if she makes a sound.

Biddy shuts her eyes
to hold back her tears.
She has no taste
for corn that season.

When fall comes,
another enslaved woman,
Hannah, and her three children
join the Smiths' household.
Biddy and Hannah
become like sisters,
and their children
like cousins.

One afternoon
a few men come
to visit the Smiths.

Biddy and Hannah
are shucking corn,
and Biddy overhears
them talking about
moving to a place called
 "Great Salt Lake City."

Like green husk,
Biddy and her children
can easily be ripped away
from one another—
even the baby growing inside her.

Biddy worries,
Are we going to be sold?

Sassafras boosts immunity, and the
leaves, bark, and roots of the tree
can be used in cooking.

SASSAFRAS

THE ECONOMY OF SLAVERY

Imagine being taken from your family one day, never to see them again, and sold to people you do not know miles and miles away from the place you call home. Enslaved African Americans described this experience as being "stolen." After 1808, when the Trans-Atlantic Slave Trade was abolished in the United States, children born into slavery in this country were a necessary part of keeping the slave trade going.

A SLAVE FATHER SOLD AWAY FROM HIS FAMILY.

Being sold was a traumatic event for enslaved families, as this 1860 print of a father being sold away from his family shows.

HAVE YOU EVER BEEN TAKEN AWAY FROM SOMEONE YOU LOVE?

This embroidered cloth bag is known as "Ashley's Sack." It was given to nine-year-old Ashley when she was sold away from her mother, Rose, in the mid-1800s. Rose filled the cottonseed sack with a dress, three handful of pecans, a braid of her hair, and "my love always." Ashley never saw her mother again. It was Ashley's granddaughter, Ruth Middleton, who stitched the story onto the sack in 1921. "Ashley's Sack" is on display at the National Museum of African American History and Culture in Washington, DC.

My great grandmother Rose
mother of Ashley gave her this sack when
she was sold at age 9 in South Carolina
it held a tattered dress 3 handfulls of
pecans a braid of Roses hair. Told her
It be filled with my Love always
she never saw her again
Ashley is my grandmother
Ruth Middleton
1921

Biddy was forced to move when she became the property of Robert and Rebecca Smith (pictured here). No one today knows why or how. Sometime in the 1840s, the Smiths moved Biddy and her daughters to Tishomingo County, Mississippi, to live on their tenant farm. Biddy's new mistress, Rebecca, was often ill, which might explain why they wanted to own Biddy, who had healing skills.

Eventually the Smiths bought Hannah, who had been enslaved in Rebecca's childhood household. At around twenty-five years old, Hannah was brought to the farm with her three children. This act separated Hannah from Frank, her partner and father of her children.

Biddy's life in the Smiths' two-room cabin would have been different from her experience on a larger slave plantation. With fewer people to help on a tenant farm, Biddy would have had more responsibilities. In addition to laboring in the field, she would have cleared land and done various household chores like cooking and laundering clothes. Robert and Rebecca Smith, who were members of the Mormon church, eventually decided to move to what was then called Great Salt Lake City in what would become the state of Utah. A group of Mormons was going there to start a new community.

The Smiths didn't have much money, and their home might have looked like this house pictured on a tenant farm in Mississippi.

TENANT FARMER: a person who farms on land owned by another person, and pays the landowner an agreed-upon fee in money, crops, or both.

MORMON: a member of the Church of Jesus Christ of Latter-Day Saints (LDS), often referred to as the Mormon church. Since the Mormons faced religious discrimination and violence in the eastern United States, leader Brigham Young established a new community out West in the Utah Territory.

Naming Practices as Cultural Memory

Enslaved people continued the African tradition of naming children in honor of loved ones. This naming practice is a way of linking the past to the present and keeping alive the memory of loved ones. Female children were often given the first names of their grandmothers.

In the case of Biddy, we know her daughters' names were Ellen, Ann, and Harriet. So when we created the Granny Ellen character, we thought that Biddy might have named her eldest daughter after her granny. As for last names, enslaved people would be given or would take the name of the master, or they would make up their own last names. It was common for enslaved people to be referred to in the possessive, as objects, like "Robert Smith's Biddy."

The system of slavery was woven into all the parts of the United States, and people across the country benefited from it. Slave owners made money from the work of enslaved people. Slave traders made money from the people they sold. Owners of ships and railroads made money trafficking humans across water and land. Enslaved people built roads, dams, homes, and public buildings. The United States became a wealthy, prosperous country because of the labor of enslaved people.

SLAVE TRADER: a person who buys, transports, and sells human beings as slaves.

HUMAN TRAFFICKING: buying and selling human beings to others for the purpose of forced physical and/or sexual labor.

ECONOMY: a community or nation's system for producing, selling, buying, and using resources and services.

WAMSUTTA MILLS.

Slavery existed in all of the Northern states until being outlawed or slowly stopped over time. But Northern economies continued to run on slavery and racism. New England mills and factories, such as the Wamsutta Mills in Massachusetts, made cloth from the cotton enslaved people were forced to pick. This cotton cloth was turned into clothing, bedding, and other necessities that all Americans bought and used.

By 1860, close to 4 million enslaved people were worth more than 3.5 billion dollars— the most valuable single asset in the United States.

Enslaved people built the White House.

It is difficult to know the paternity of Biddy's children. Records show that Biddy most likely lived with the Smiths by the time her youngest daughter, Harriet, was born. This suggests that Harriet might have been fathered by Robert Smith. Enslaved women could sometimes partner and have children with enslaved men. Masters could also rape enslaved women. Enslaved people did not have a choice about how their bodies were used, since they were seen as property.

Isaac White and Rosina Downs (pictured here) were both enslaved because their mothers were enslaved. This is because slavery was matrilineal, which meant that if a mother was enslaved, her child was born enslaved. When White masters raped enslaved women, the children born from those pregnancies were often enslaved by their own fathers and added to their fathers' wealth.

Enslaved women and girls spun thread, weaved, and quilted as part of their unpaid work. They made "scrap quilts" for their families with leftover materials and worn clothes, learning and sharing patterns as well as developing their own creative designs. Some quilts depicted folklore and biblical stories. Some told family stories, like this quilt made by Harriet Powers that tells of her life enslaved. Artists today, such as Faith Ringgold, continue to use quilts to pass stories from one generation to the next.

TIMELINE

1838
October 15
Biddy's daughter Ellen is born.

1840
The US Census records a total population of 17,069,453, including 2,487,355 enslaved people and 386,293 free Black people.

1842–1843
Biddy's daughter Ann is born.

1846
Hannah and her children are bought by the Smiths.

1847
Biddy's daughter Harriet is born.

WHERE DO THE THINGS YOU BUY AND USE COME FROM, AND HOW ARE THEY MADE?

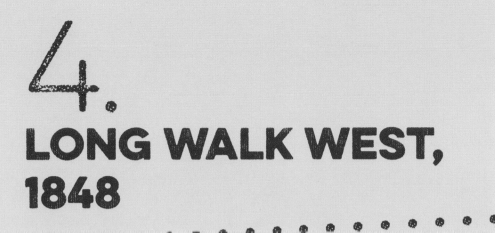

4.
LONG WALK WEST, 1848

Not sold after all,
Biddy coos to Harriet,
her newborn,
securely wrapped
to her back.

She coaxes
five-year-old Ann
and nine-year-old Ellen
to keep going,
as they walk
behind the Smiths'
three covered wagons
and livestock.

Ten never-ending hours
each day, in pouring rains
that turn trails muddy,
they walk.

Biddy is responsible for
keeping two yoke of oxen,
eight mules, and seven
cows on course.
She pulls the mules
out of mud, pushes wagon
wheels out of ditches.

On a ferry ride
on the Mississippi River,
Biddy wonders,
How many of us crossed
this River to freedom?

Hannah gives birth
to a baby girl,
who Biddy helps
deliver beneath
a bright North Star.

They reach shore,
and walk for a month
to Winter Quarters.
On Potawatomi land,
they rest their blistered
and callused feet.

Biddy searches the fields
to make her medicines.
But she doesn't recognize
most of the plants
in this new place.

Through the gauzy
light of an early May

morning, she hears
singing coming from
the black chokecherries.

Biddy walks around
the shrubs and encounters
a Potawatomi woman
digging up roots.

They speak through plants—
with gestures and signs,
with their open hands.

Walking together
along the Elkhorn River,
the woman points out
a plant with broad leaves
and white flowers.

"Wapsepenik," she says,
and shows Biddy the roots
and tells her to pound them
into a pulp to heal
the sores on her feet.

Later that night,
after Biddy serves
the Smiths their
mush-and-milk dinner
and washes their dishes,
Biddy tells her daughters
about the Potawatomi
woman who knew plants
like their Granny Ellen.

As the campfires twinkle
on the open plains, Biddy
applies the wapsepenik poultice
to her girls' feet.

She tells them Granny Ellen
was about Ellen's age
when a neighboring
tribe raided her village.
They kidnapped her
and sold her into slavery.

As Biddy braids Ann's hair,
she says, "They forced Granny
to walk and walk
from inland to shore...."

She finishes Ann's hair
and begins to nurse
Harriet to sleep.
"Granny knew no one
on the ships
that brought her here."

Ellen asks,
"Not even her mama?"

"Not even her mama
or sisters came with her
to this new world," Biddy says.

WAPSEPENIK

The roots of the wapsepenik, also
known as wild calla, can be made
into a poultice to relieve soreness
and swelling.

PASSAGES

Biddy, Hannah, and their seven children were forced to go west with the Smiths in a wagon train of ninety people, thirty-four of them enslaved. In addition to serving the Smiths, Biddy had to take care of her own young children while also tending to the livestock.

This mass migration of Mormons was part of a larger westward expansion and colonization taking place at the time. By 1840, almost seven million Americans had moved west to seek land, opportunities, and better lives. But hundreds of distinct tribal communities already called the North American continent their home. New settlers violently forced Native people off the land to claim it for themselves.

WAGON TRAIN: a group of wagons travelling together over land, often with supplies for a group of settlers.

MIGRATION: movement to another place, often of a large group of people or animals.

WESTWARD EXPANSION: the expansion of United States–controlled territory westward, from the Atlantic Ocean in the East to the Pacific Ocean in the West.

COLONIZATION: one group's act of forcibly taking control over a territory and/or group, often through violence. The United States colonized North America by murdering and forcefully removing Native people from their homelands.

Their route took them across Tennessee and Kentucky, on a steamboat up the Mississippi River, then across Missouri. They trudged through rain, mud, floods, and ice. Most people traveled this difficult journey on foot and walked nearly one thousand miles total to Winter Quarters.

Potawatomi Indians permitted the Mormons, who were escaping persecution for their religious beliefs, to stop and rest on tribal land in what is now North Omaha, Nebraska.

The Mormons called this stopping place Winter Quarters. They rested here before taking the last part of their journey to Great Salt Lake City. Biddy, Hannah, and their children spent about a month here, where Biddy would have searched for local plant medicines.

This is a sketch of an Indiana Potawatomi woman in the 1830s.

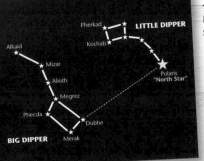

Many enslaved people escaped slavery in the Southern states to free states in the north and west, and also to Canada. Under the secret cover of night, those crossing the Mississippi and Ohio Rivers used the North Star as a guide. They found the North Star by connecting the stars of the Big Dipper constellation, which enslaved African Americans called the Drinking Gourd. The outermost stars that make up the Gourd point to Polaris, the North Star.

The Middle Passage was the second, or middle, leg of the Trans-Atlantic Slave Trade, the triangular voyage between Europe, Africa, and the Americas. The Middle Passage was the crossing of the Atlantic Ocean by enslaved people, a quarter of them children.

From the 1520s to the 1860s, an estimated 12.5 million African women, children, and men were captured, put on European slave ships, and carried across the Atlantic Ocean.

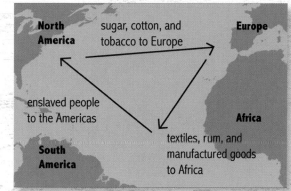

People were packed below decks, often locked in irons, barely able to move, and kept naked or partially clothed. Many died along the way from sickness, bad food, and abuse. During the years of the Trans-Atlantic Slave Trade, between nine and ten million people survived this terrible journey. Slave traders in the Americas and Caribbean bought those who survived the crossing.

TIMELINE

1808
The Trans-Atlantic Slave Trade ends for the United States, but domestic trade continues.

1830
May 28
President Andrew Jackson signs the Indian Removal Act.

1848
March 17
Biddy, Hannah, their children, and the Smiths leave Mississippi.

April
Hannah's fourth child, Jane, is born.

May 17
Their wagon train arrives at Winter Quarters.

5.
COTTONWOOD, UTAH

After five more grueling
months of walking,
they finally arrive
at the Great Salt Lake,
covered high in snow,
in silent cotton tears.

They settle in a town
called Cottonwood.
The Smiths scramble to cut
down trees to build one log cabin
where all of them will sleep.

That winter, November's
freeze grips hard and their
provisions grow low.

Taking inventory of their supplies,
Biddy says, "Not enough
flour to make biscuits,
not enough food."

She bundles up and knocks
on her neighbor's door.

The warmth of Jane James's
home rushes toward Biddy
when the door opens.
She and her husband, two sons,
and newborn Mary Ann
are a few of the free Black people in town.

Jane offers Biddy
two pounds of cornmeal,
half of what she has.
Biddy is grateful for her generosity—
for giving with an open hand
when she doesn't have much to give.

A week later,
there's a knock on the Smiths' door.
Jane is frightened—Mary Ann
has a fever and wet cough.

"I can help," Biddy says,
and Jane relaxes with relief.

Biddy mixes up
a mustard plaster
to draw the congestion
from Mary Ann's chest.

The baby kicks her feet
when Biddy applies it.
It's a blessing for Biddy
to use Granny Ellen's remedies

on a free Black child—
a free Black body.

"What's it like to be free?"
Biddy asks Jane.

"There's a comfort in knowing
no master or mistress is going
to break my family apart."
Jane cradles her baby in her arms.

"Me and my husband
work according to our
own family's needs and
priorities—not no master's."

She raises her brows,
looks Biddy in the eyes.
"With your fine skills, Biddy,
there's no saying what you could do."

The seeds of the mustard plant can be
made into a plaster and used to draw
congestion from the chest.

MUSTARD

SEEING FREEDOM

Biddy, Hannah, their children, and the Smiths covered nearly one thousand more miles as the wagon train moved from Winter Quarters to Great Salt Lake City. The last one hundred miles were the hardest, with mountains to climb and little grass for cattle to eat. They arrived at Great Salt Lake City in October 1848. By this time, around fifty Black people lived among the seventeen hundred who had settled in the Salt Lake Valley. Around half were enslaved and the other half were free.

Artist Thomas Moran's 1875 painting of settlers arriving at Great Salt Lake City.

Popular Occupations Held by Free Black Women Before the Civil War

- ★ Cook
- ★ Dressmaker
- ★ Hairdresser
- ★ Housekeeper (maid)
- ★ Laundress
- ★ Nurse
- ★ Midwife
- ★ Peddler
- ★ Seamstress
- ★ Staying home to tend their own children and house

Jane Elizabeth Manning James was born free in Connecticut and came to Great Salt Lake City after joining the Mormon religion. She was the first Black woman to enter the Utah Territory in 1847, and her daughter Mary Ann was the first Black child to be born there. We made up these scenes in which Jane James and Biddy interact. Considering they lived in a small community, where enslaved and free Black people built friendships and shared resources, they probably helped each other.

WHAT DOES FREEDOM MEAN TO YOU?

How Could Black People Be Legally Free During This Time?

★ They were born free as children of legally free women.

★ They used the Underground Railroad, the "freedom train," to escape enslavement. The Underground Railroad was not a real train. It was a secret network of people and places that helped people travel to freedom without being captured—from Southern slave states to free states in the North and West, and also into Canada and Mexico. From the early 1800s until the Civil War, an estimated 100,000 people escaped on the Railroad.

★ They were set free voluntarily by slave owners. This was known as manumission.

★ They sued for their freedom in court. In 1783, Quock Walker fought in the state supreme court for his freedom because the Massachusetts Declaration of Rights said that "all men are born equal and free." The court decided in Walker's favor, and slavery was abolished in Massachusetts. Walker had fought for justice and won. But using the court system was an uphill struggle for people without money or power, and courts did not consistently apply the law in a fair way.

★ They bought their freedom from their masters or mistresses. This was called "self-purchase," and was very rare. Often enslaved people who had this opportunity earned money from skilled labor like carpentry, shoemaking, dressmaking, or midwifery, and their masters let them keep some of the money for themselves. Once freed, they received manumission papers, also known as freedom papers.

SUE: take a legal action against a person or institution.

COURT: a meeting place for people who need a law-related judgment or decision.

STATE SUPREME COURT: the highest court in a state.

JUSTICE: fairness.

Manumission certificate written by Philip Winebrenner for James Tooley from 1828 in Maryland.

TIMELINE

1847
September
Jane James enters the Utah Territory.

1848
May
Jane James's daughter Mary Ann is born.

October 19
Biddy, Hannah, and their children arrive at Great Salt Lake City.

1850
The US Census lists 50 Black people in Utah, 24 free and 26 enslaved.

6.
CALIFORNIA DREAMING

Spring arrives and grasshoppers
eat everything—plow handles,
vegetable crops, the herbs Biddy
planted for teas and medicines.

Biddy and her daughters
are hanging clothes to dry
when their friend Lizzy Rowan
drops by and brings word that a group
of Mormons are going to California.

Her mistress plans to move
Lizzy to the new colony.
According to Lizzy,
who traveled too from Mississippi,
California is a free state.

Biddy thanks Lizzy for this news.
She wonders, *Could this be
the path to a free life
for me and my girls?*

Three months later,
150 wagons move along
like ants in single file toward
San Bernardino, California.

Biddy's daughters have grown
walking across this country.
Ellen, once frightened by
black clouds of buffalo, squints
her thirteen-year-old eyes against dust.
Ann is eight, and stubborn
like the Rocky Mountains.
They've seen prairie grass taller
than Harriet is now, at three.

Together, they face the Mojave Desert.
Its heat beats out their sweat, says:
"You do not belong here."
There's not enough water to go around.

Biddy stumbles.
She remembers long-ago
Sunday mornings, the cool
canopy of oaks and pines,
looking for plants.

She hears Granny Ellen's
earthy voice singing:
I lost my soul in the wilderness;
I'm a-going home....

Before Biddy's eyes,
a mirage of Granny appears.
Biddy wipes sweat off her brow,
blinks to make sure she's seeing clearly.

Granny's hair is wrapped in royal blue
and her body is draped in honey-colored cloth.
She rocks in a chair, on a porch,
surrounded by a picket fence.
Her smile quenches Biddy's thirst.

Granny Ellen beckons to Biddy
and says, "Just keep putting
one foot in front of the other.
You are going home."

A gunshot rings through the air
startling Biddy. She and her girls link hands.

An ox too weak to stand
was shot dead. By nightfall,
it will be covered in sand.

"Come on, my children,"
Biddy says, with her eyes
on the thistle-dotted hillsides.
"One foot in front of the other."

Thistle symbolizes bravery, endurance, and determination. It stands for surviving where others won't and withstanding harsh conditions. In a tincture, it can help remove toxins from the body.

THISTLE

REMAINING RESILIENT

In 1851, 437 members of the Great Salt Lake community, including 26 Black people, moved to Southern California to establish a new Mormon colony or settlement. Biddy, Hannah, and their children were part of the group, as was Hannah's enslaved partner, Toby Embers, who was also the father of Hannah's fifth child, Charles. They all had to endure the long and difficult journey, walking for miles and looking after livestock, even in the punishing desert.

RESILIENCE: behaviors, thoughts, and actions that are learned and developed to recover from hard times, trauma, and great stress.

COLONY or SETTLEMENT: a place or region that is newly settled by people who didn't originally live there. Usually the new arrivals in a settlement keep the cultural practices and traditions of their place of origin.

RECREATION: activity that gives a person or people new life, energy, or encouragement.

SPIRITUAL: relating to the spirit or soul.

Nourishing the Spirit

In addition to taking care of their bodies in difficult and stressful situations, enslaved people learned how to nourish their spirits. Believing in something greater than themselves helped them to identify with more than just their enslavement. They found a power within that restored their humanity. Some creative spiritual practices included fellowship, dancing, storytelling, laughter, quilting, and singing.

Spirituals, work songs, and recreational songs, such as "I'm Going Home," gave enslaved African Americans spiritual and emotional support through the hardships of slavery. Singing eased the toil of back-breaking labor. It was a way of communicating, expressing feelings, and imagining life beyond enslavement.

WHAT KEEPS YOUR MIND, BODY, AND SPIRIT GOING?

Seventeen-year-old Elizabeth (Lizzy) Flake Rowan (pictured here) had been part of the "Mississippi Mormon" group that came to Great Salt Lake City with Biddy three years earlier. Lizzy would become a key member of the Black community in San Bernardino, California, where she worked as a laundress. Her daughter, Alice Rowan Johnson, was one of the first Black people to graduate from college in California in 1888, and she became a teacher herself.

As the United States expanded to the west, politicians and state governments argued about whether the newly forming states would be slave states or free states. In 1848 the United States won the Mexican American War, taking over new territory and displacing Native and Mexican people who lived in what would become California. California entered the country as a free state in 1850.

In this map, red states are "free states," where slavery was illegal. Blue states are "slave states," where slavery was legal. The areas in green were unresolved territories.

DISPLACE: to force someone from their home or homeland.

FUGITIVE: a person who escapes from a place, often in secret, to avoid the law.

BOUNTY HUNTER: a person who tracks down fugitives and returns them for a monetary reward.

Lawmakers passed the Fugitive Slave Act in 1850. This law said that enslaved people who had escaped to free states were no longer safe. They could be recaptured by bounty hunters, brought back to slave states in the South, and resold into slavery, as this image shows. If Biddy ran away, she could be returned to her master. Free Black people could also be captured. If they didn't have freedom papers on them, they could be sold into slavery, even though they were free.

TIMELINE

1846–1848
The Mexican-American War.

1848
January 24
Gold is discovered in California.

1850
September 8
California joins the United States as a free state.

September 18
The Fugitive Slave Act is passed.

1851
March 24
Biddy, Hannah, and their children leave the Great Salt Lake.

7.
FREEDOM
FOR SOME

For now, the freedom
Biddy can give her daughters
is a walk in the woodlands
to pick juniper berries
alongside the Santa Ana River.

Smith is still keeping them
enslaved. Their labor makes
him a successful cattle rancher.

Careful not to crush
the berries between her fingers,
Biddy thinks, *If I leave*
it up to Master Smith,
we'll never be free.
But she can't risk trying to escape.

For four years, they've been
on the ranch, Biddy doing
what's she told. Her chores
include shopping for the Smiths

in nearby Los Angeles. There,
she meets more free Black people.

Biddy becomes friends
with Bob and Winnie Owens.
Enslaved in Texas, Bob purchased
freedom for himself and his family.

The Owens own a corral
on San Pedro Street.
Vaqueros help Bob
sell horses to settlers
seeking a new life in California.

The Owens' son Charles
and Biddy's daughter Ellen
are sweet on each other.

Biddy watches Ellen pause
from picking juniper berries
to smell the sagebrush.
Sometimes, out in these woods,
Biddy feels the urge
to talk with Granny Ellen.

"Can you believe
your granddaughter is
seventeen years old,
and with a heart
opened to love?"

A breeze brushes Biddy's face soft.
She calls out for her daughters
and they head back to the Smiths'.

They set the baskets full of berries
on the kitchen floor.
Smith comes in,
jaw clenched.
He tells Biddy he's selling
half the cattle and moving them to Texas.
Biddy pulls Ellen, Ann, and Harriet close.
In Texas, they'll never have
a chance at freedom.

A few days later,
Smith drops Biddy off
at the trading post in Los Angeles
to buy supplies for the trip.
Biddy bumps into Charles Owens.

She pulls him aside.
"He plans to take us to Texas,"
she tells him quietly.
"Said we'd be just as free
there as we are here."

"What?" Charles gasps.
"I'll never see Ellen again."

"I know," Biddy whispers.
"I didn't come to no free state
to have us walked back into slavery—
worked like mules, and my girls
forced to be breeding women."

Biddy takes hold of his hand.
"I told Lizzy Rowan about this too."

Then, her gut tells her
to gather up the supplies.

"Charles, we are
not to go to Texas."

Within seconds, Smith shouts,
"Biddy, load the wagon!"
And she sees her plan
take shape in Charles's eyes.

A rich source of vitamin C, juniper
berries, which are actually female
seed cones, can be used dried or
fresh, whole or crushed, to flavor
meat dishes or to make a sauce or
marinade.

JUNIPER

IN A FREE STATE BUT NOT FREE

Biddy and her family arrived in San Bernardino, where Robert Smith established a successful cattle ranch. He would have known that slavery was illegal in California, but he continued to hold Biddy, Hannah, and their children captive for four years. After Mormon leaders took over his ranch because it was so successful, Robert Smith decided to move everyone to Texas where slavery was legal.

Some sources say that Biddy told Charles Owens and Lizzy Rowan they were leaving. Even though she and her children legally should have been free, Biddy didn't have the power to challenge Robert Smith on her own.

San Bernardino, 1850s.

A dry goods store in Los Angeles, 1870. In preparation for the move, Robert Smith sold some of his cattle and purchased supplies at a store like this.

HOW CAN YOU AND YOUR FRIENDS SUPPORT ONE ANOTHER AND THOSE FACING INJUSTICE?

Legal Injustice

It was written in California's state constitution that "Neither slavery nor involuntary servitude unless for the punishment of crimes shall ever be tolerated in this state." But this freedom was rarely enforced. When slave owners realized that local authorities didn't care about the law, they continued to hold people captive, and slavery continued. It was against the law for a person who wasn't White to testify in court against a White person. This meant that if enslaved people did challenge slave owners in court cases, they could not testify and usually lost.

There was one group that could be legally enslaved in California: California's Native people. A law in 1850, called "An Act for the Government and Protection of Indians," allowed a judge to declare an unemployed Native person to be a "vagrant." That person could then be sold and forced to work for no pay for up to four months. It was also legal for Native children to be indentured to White families until they grew up.

Bounty hunters kidnapped and sold Native children into this kind of slavery.

The boy pictured here was from the Maidu tribal nation, and some sources say he was forced to work as a nanny in California. This law was part of a statewide effort to remove Native people from their lands, and to separate a generation of young people and adults from their languages and cultures.

Robert (Bob) and Winnie Owens were enslaved in Texas until they managed to save enough money to buy their freedom. The family, including their three children, moved to Los Angeles in the early 1850s. At the time, there were fewer than 20 Black people living in a city of about 3,500 people. In such a small community, African Americans knew and supported each other in whatever ways they could.

ENFORCE: to make sure that people do what is required by law.

AUTHORITIES: people in positions of power to enforce laws, or who have the power to influence or command thought, opinion, or behavior.

TESTIFY: to give a formal written or spoken statement in court.

CASE: a law-related disagreement.

JUDGE: a government official who is given the power to supervise and make decisions in legal cases.

VAGRANT: a person without a steady home and regular work who wanders from place to place.

INDENTURED: being under contract to work for another person for no money, usually in exchange for passage to a new place, or for a set amount of time.

Robert Owens built a successful business selling cattle and horses. He hired free Black people and Mexican American *vaqueros*, or cowboys, to work with him. Los Angeles was still a small, dusty town when Robert Owens bought his first property in 1854. He eventually owned an entire city block. Robert and Winnie's son Charles and Biddy's daughter Ellen fell in love. This would be the beginning of a long connection between Biddy and the Owens family.

This series of drawings shows Los Angeles in 1857.

The first cowboys in California were Mexican American *vaqueros*, from the Spanish word for "cow." Charles Owens worked with *vaqueros* who had lived in California when it was still colonized by Mexico. Black cowboys like Charles made a living working as cattle herders, cooks, and ranchers, and played an important part in Western history.

TIMELINE

1850
California has nearly 1,000 Black residents; by 1852 this doubled to 2,000. The US Census shows around 3.2 million people enslaved across the nation.

An Act for the Government and Protection of Indians is passed.

1851
June 9
Biddy, Hannah, and their children arrive in San Bernardino, California.

Fall 1855
Robert Smith decides to move to Texas.

8.
HOPE

The stars shine
bright as lanterns.
Coyotes howl in the hills
as the trail hands ride
their horses in circles,
guarding the cattle.
On their way to Texas,
Biddy and her family camp
in the Santa Monica Canyon.

The cold wind bites,
and the campfire can't
warm Biddy's bones.

Robert Smith paces
back and forth
and reacts to every
rustle in the chaparral,
his finger ready
on the trigger.

When Biddy hears
the thuds of horses
galloping toward

the camp, she stops
with the cleaning.

Smith pulls out his gun.
His sons and hired men
aim their rifles
at the pitch-dark night.

Biddy runs
to wake Hannah
and the children.

A man emerges
on his horse,
a silver star gleaming
on his chest.

Smith lowers his shotgun.
In the background
there are more men
whose faces are hard
for Biddy to see.

The man with the star
says he's Sheriff Alexander.
He hands Smith
a piece of paper, says
it's a "habeas corpus."

Smith reads it
by the fire's glow.
Pointing in Biddy's direction,
the sheriff orders
his men to "take them
into protective custody."

Biddy quickly pushes
her daughters behind her
back and braces herself
for the two men
stepping from the night.

She whispers, "My Word"
upon recognizing Bob
and Charles Owens.
"I'm glad to see it's you."

They escort Hannah,
the children, and Biddy
to the sheriff's wagon.

As the wheels take them
from Smith's scowling face,
Biddy peers into a darkness
as rich as soil. She sees
her freedom growing.

PATHS OF RESISTANCE

In late December, Biddy, Hannah, and their ten children, the Smiths and their seven children, and some hired trail hands moved to the Santa Monica hills. The night they camped out in 1855, it was a freezing 33 degrees: "The coldest we have ever experienced," a church clerk in San Bernardino reported.

Chaparral covers the Santa Monica hills. Made up of shrubs and small trees, it is California's most extensive native plant community.

Even though Biddy was legally free, she had to rely on her community to support her in resisting Robert Smith and the institution of slavery. It is not known for sure who reported Robert Smith's plan to take Biddy out of California. Later, Robert and Charles Owens said they did it, while Biddy's daughter Ellen mentioned Lizzy Rowan. What we do know is that in late December, Sheriff Clift and Sheriff Alexander asked Judge Benjamin Hayes to sign a writ of habeas corpus.

The Latin words *habeas corpus* literally mean "you have the body." Since the 1600s in England, this has become a legal term that protects people from unjust imprisonment. The United States Constitution says that no one should be held in prison without due process. Biddy, Hannah, and their children were being taken to a state where they would not be free, which was a form of unfair imprisonment. Robert Smith had to go to court to say why it was just to take them to Texas.

Acts of Resistance

For as long as Black people were enslaved, they resisted slavery. Just as Biddy relied on help from her community to fight for her freedom, enslaved people supported each other in acts of resistance, small and large, to build a culture of resilience.

EVERYDAY ACTS OF RESISTANCE: These actions happened daily and on a massive scale. They included working slowly, destroying equipment, learning and teaching one another to read, using plants as birth control to limit how many babies enslaved women would have, and poisoning slave owners through food preparation and medicines.

This portrait of Nat Turner was painted by African American artist Lorenzo Harris in 1936.

NAT TURNER'S REBELLION: In 1831, in Southampton County, Virginia, the enslaved preacher Nat Turner led the largest revolt of enslaved Black people in United States history. It lasted for three nights, and fifty-seven White people were killed. After the rebels were captured, over one hundred were executed, including Nat Turner. Nat Turner's rebellion destroyed the myth that enslaved people were happy being enslaved, which is how some people justified slavery.

HARRIET TUBMAN AND THE UNDERGROUND RAILROAD: Abolitionist Harriet Tubman escaped slavery and repeatedly risked her life returning to help enslaved African Americans escape to freedom. Tubman became a successful conductor of the Underground Railroad, taking nineteen trips to the South between 1850 and 1860, and freeing more than three hundred women, men, and children, including her entire family. Later, Tubman would serve as a spy and military leader, helping the Union Army win the Civil War.

RESISTANCE: refusal to accept or go along with something, and to take action against it.

REVOLT: to rebel and take violent action against those in power.

EXECUTE: when a government or self-appointed authority kills someone on purpose, often for a stated reason.

JUSTIFY: to show or prove to be right and fair.

ABOLITIONIST: a person who fights for the end of slavery.

TIMELINE

1831
Nat Turner's Rebellion.

1850–1860
Harriet Tubman is active within the Underground Railroad.

December 1855
Biddy and others camp in the Santa Monica hills.

Late December
Biddy, Hannah, and their children are taken from the camp.

WHO IS RESISTING INJUSTICE TODAY, AND WHAT CAN YOU DO TO SUPPORT THEM?

9.
VERDICT, 1856

There will be a trial.
Robert Smith is accused
of taking Biddy, Hannah,
and their children
by force from California.

*And we're the ones
behind bars,* Biddy thinks.

She sleeps on a cot,
goes to the bathroom
using a chamber pot.
The Owens visit,
bring them food
and clean clothes.

Never this long
has Biddy gone without
wandering the woods, her feet
praying with the earth.

First enslaved,
and now imprisoned.

There's so much law between
Biddy and her freedom.

At the trial,
Smith tells Judge Hayes
that Biddy is
a member of his family
and willingly chose to
go with him to Texas.

The courtroom is packed.
Members of the
Colored Conventions
shake their heads
in disbelief when Smith
claims that he
doesn't control Biddy
any more than he controls
his own children.

The trial will determine
if this is true.

Judge Hayes is White.
The jury is White. A White
lawyer must speak for
Biddy and her family.

It's been twenty-two days
they have spent in the jail.
The second day of the trial,
Biddy's lawyer doesn't show up.

So Judge Hayes interviews
Biddy and the oldest children
inside his chambers.

He asks Biddy if she's
controlled by Robert Smith.
In her head, Biddy sees
Granny Ellen whipped.

"I have always done
what I have been told
to do," Biddy begins.

She closes her eyes
and her people's suffering
hasn't gone away.

She takes a deep breath.
Then a second breath.

"I always feared
this trip to Texas,
since I first heard of it...."

Judge Hayes tells Biddy
if she chooses Texas,
her children will not go
with her. They cannot
be taken to a slave state
and lose their freedom.

Biddy finds her courage,
strong as an oak
in the center of her chest.

She opens her eyes,
looks directly at Judge Hayes,
and Biddy speaks:

"I do not wish
to be separated
from my children,
and do not in such
a case wish to go."

Biddy and the others
return to the courtroom.
The gallery is silent as a sunrise.

When Judge Hayes
bangs his gavel, declaring
that Biddy and her family
are "free forever,"
the crowd bursts
into a new day.

The California poppy, which appears in illustrations throughout this book, is the official state flower and a native wildflower of California. Spanish colonizers called the plant the "Cup of Gold." Made into a tincture, it cleanses wounds and helps with pain and sleep problems.

POPPY

60

SPEAKING UP

The sheriff's wagons took Biddy, Hannah, and their ten children to the county jail on Spring and Franklin Streets, behind the Los Angeles courthouse. Then, on January 1, 1856, Judge Hayes called Robert Smith to his chambers to respond to the charges. Smith said that Biddy and Hannah "left Mississippi with their own consent, rather than remain there," and that "he has supported them ever since, subjecting them to no greater control than his own children, and not holding them as slaves." The way Smith explained it, Biddy, Hannah, and their children were family to him, not enslaved, and they were freely choosing to go with the Smiths to Texas.

The first Los Angeles jail.

Judge Hayes had to figure out the truth. On January 15, Biddy's lawyer didn't appear. Because she was not White, Biddy could not speak directly in court against a White person. Smith's lawyer demanded that the case be stopped. Instead, Judge Hayes made the decision to call Biddy, Hannah, and their eldest children into his chambers.

Judge Hayes later wrote a newspaper article about the trial. He wrote down what he said were Biddy's answers, but not his questions. He said that he explained to Biddy that if she said she wanted to go to Texas, she could not take her children. The children would be unjustly imprisoned in a slave state. The answer he wrote from her was clear: "I do not wish to be separated from my children, and do not in such a case wish to go."

Judge Benjamin Hayes around 1848.

HOW CAN YOU SPEAK UP WHEN YOU ARE AFRAID OR FEEL LIKE YOU DON'T HAVE POWER?

We will never know exactly what Biddy and Judge Hayes said during this interview, but we do know that Biddy's responses helped him to make his ruling that legally freed Biddy, Hannah, and their children. When Biddy bravely spoke up for herself and her children, her actions impacted the larger struggle for African American rights.

RULING: an official decision, especially one made by a judge.

UNITED STATES SUPREME COURT: the highest court in our country, ruled by nine appointed judges, also known as justices.

CITIZEN: a person who belongs to a country, according to the law, and has the rights and protections of that country.

The Dred Scott Decision

Biddy was lucky that her case took place before 1857, when the case of *Dred Scott v. Sandford* was decided by the United States Supreme Court. The court ruled that because Scott was Black and a descendant of slaves, he was not, and could never be, an American citizen. This meant that even though he was taken to a free state, he could not sue for his freedom. Many people think this was one of the worst decisions made by the United States Supreme Court.

DRED SCOTT

TIMELINE

1830
September
The First Colored Convention is held in Philadelphia.

1855
November
The First California Colored Convention in Sacramento.

1856
January 1
The preliminary hearing in Biddy's case is held in Judge Hayes's chambers.

Coming Together to Fight for Change

People involved in the Colored Conventions held gatherings all over the country, including in California. Representatives from Black churches, social clubs, and other organizations gathered at four California Colored Conventions that took place between 1855 and 1865. The first was held in Sacramento a month before Biddy Mason's trial, and some say that members called for the sheriff to stop Smith from taking Biddy and her family to Texas.

People going to these conventions raised money to hire lawyers to speak up against discrimination. They focused on fighting for the right of Black people to testify in court. They also fought for the right to vote, for equality in education, and on behalf of people still enslaved in the state. Through these conventions, Black people organized as a movement to fight for the rights of all Black people in the state.

Proceedings cover page, 1855.

This illustration is from the 1869 Colored Convention in Washington, DC.

COLORED: the term preferred by Black or African American people to describe themselves during Biddy's lifetime. This has shifted to "Negro," "Afro American," and now "Black" or "African American." "Colored" today is an offensive term. Always ask people how they choose to identify.

DISCRIMINATION: the act of treating a person or group unfairly because of what they look like, what they believe, or for other reasons related to their perceived identity.

MOVEMENT: a group of people working together to advance their shared political, social, or artistic ideas.

January 14
Smith's trial begins.

January 19
Judge Hayes legally frees Biddy, Hannah, and their children.

1857
The Dred Scott decision is made.

1863
California abolishes the rule that Black people cannot testify against White people in court.

10.
LIVING FREE

Biddy enters the kitchen
glowing and thankful,
with a sunny "Good morning."

She looks around the Owens' table
at Ellen, who will soon marry Charles,
Ann, who helps her catch babies now,
and little Harriet, who at only eight years old
got a job with a local family.

There are Winnie and Bob,
who have opened their home
to them, and Biddy is grateful
for all their care and support.

Biddy sits next to Winnie and Harriet.
Eggs and toast waiting for her,
she asks to lead everyone in grace.
The Masons and Owens join
hands and bow their heads.

"Thank you, Lord,
for the food we're about to eat,

for the land from which it came,
for the people who work the fields..."

After Judge Hayes's ruling,
Biddy immediately began
working for herself
as a midwife and nurse.
She's seen carrying her black nursing bag
throughout all of Los Angeles.

With clients like Pío Pico,
no wonder her business is doing well.
The once-governor of California
uses Biddy's tonics for his joint pains,
and he is all praise.

Continuing grace, Biddy says,
"Thank you for those who have passed on,
for those we had to leave behind,
and thank you for the ones not yet born..."

She delivers the babies
of wealthy *Californios* in grand
adobes. She speaks in the Spanish
she's learning, *"Respira, señora, respira."*
And Ann is there too, supporting
the back of the expecting mother.

In the dome-shaped home
of a Tongva family,
Biddy is taught
to boil white sage roots
to make a drink that helps
mothers heal after giving birth.

"Thank you for this beautiful home,"
Biddy goes on, "that shelters
our bodies, for love keeping
us whole, for my heart, despite
it all, that remains open...."

The Masons and Owens
take a stronger hold
of each other's hands.

For her work, Biddy is now paid
in cash, in vegetables or chickens.
She saves every cent earned
for the home she'll call her own someday.

"Amen," Biddys says,
and the eight voices
around the table
reflect back to Biddy
that she is
because they are
right there with her.

White sage eases painful menstrual cramps and the symptoms of menopause faced by older women. In many Native cultures, people burn white sage in prayers and ceremonies to purify and cleanse the body and the space.

WHITE SAGE

FREE AT LAST

At thirty-seven years old, Biddy was legally free. It had taken several people acting together to help her win her case. Many others in the state did not have the money or access to power to challenge their enslavement in the courts. Those who did often lost in a system that usually sided with White people. It was truly a victory when Judge Hayes declared at the end of the trial that she and the others were free to "become settled and go to work for themselves—in peace and without fear."

The porch of the Owens' home. On the back of the photo, the number 1 is identified as being below Biddy Mason, while the number 2 is below her daughter Ellen.

A reproduction of Biddy Mason's freedom papers.

Biddy and her daughters moved into the Owens' Los Angeles home. By the end of the year, Ellen and Charles were married. Biddy's connection to the Owens family gave her support in this new life.

Biddy worked hard as a midwife, going on to deliver hundreds of babies throughout the city. She carried her black nursing bag and her freedom papers wherever she went. It was necessary to keep her freedom papers with her at all times because free Black people could be kidnapped and sold back into slavery. Around this time, Biddy started going by the last name Mason. Historian Camille Gavin, in her book *A Place of Her Own*, wrote, "Whatever [Biddy's] reasons, 'Mason' was a fitting name. The word means 'builder, a person who strengthens things.'" As a healer and midwife, Biddy built a successful career and helped strengthen the culturally diverse community of Los Angeles.

HOW HAS YOUR FAMILY WORKED TO CREATE A BETTER LIFE?

MIGRANT: a person who moves from one place to another, often in search of work and better opportunities.

The Mason, Owens, and Embers Families: A Growing Network

Prior to Biddy and her daughters' arrival, the Black population in Los Angeles included only seven women and girls. After the court case, Hannah and some of her children returned to San Bernardino, where Hannah's husband, Toby Embers, also lived. Hannah's eldest daughter, Ann, lived in Los Angeles with her husband, Manuel Pepper, who worked at the Owens' stables. They were neighbors of Biddy, her daughters, and the Owens family. The Mason, Owens, and Embers families continued to look after one another and would help to raise each others' children in this close community.

These three families became part of a growing network of Black people who looked out for one another, established businesses and social clubs, and helped new migrants to the city become settled.

This table shows reported people of different races in Los Angeles ten years after California entered the United States. The White category includes Mexican Americans.

RACE IN LOS ANGELES, 1860

	Number	Percentage
Black	87	.08%
White	9221	81.30%
Indian	2014	17.80%
Chinese	11	.10%
TOTAL	**11,333**	

Source, Historical Census Browser 1860

Los Angeles: A City of Diverse People and Cultures

The Tongva are the first people of the area now known as Los Angeles. The tribe once lived in as many as forty villages in the region, including the central village of Yang-Na.

The Spanish came to the region in 1771, building the San Gabriel Mission where they forced Native people to work and reject their cultural traditions. Mexican settlers then colonized the area in 1781 and forced Tongva people from their homes, founding the pueblo of Los Angeles north of Yang-Na. These forty-four Mexican settlers included people with Spanish, Native American, and mixed ancestry, with twenty-six of them having African ancestry.

PUEBLO: the Spanish word for "village."

AFRO-MEXICAN: Mexican citizen who is Black or of African descent.

CALIFORNIO: Person of Mexican descent who lived in California before it became part of the United States.

Tongva Nation Dancers at the Moompetam Native American Festival in 2013.

The last Mexican governor of California, Pío Pico, was Afro-Mexican. When California joined the United States in 1850, the majority of people living in Los Angeles were Spanish-speaking Californios. Some say that Biddy learned Spanish, which would have helped her build cross-cultural relationships. Biddy was reported to have had dinner at the mansion of Pío Pico, where she would have met the wealthiest residents of Los Angeles, as well as international visitors.

Pío Pico (1801–1894).

Ever since the gold rush and western expansion, people from all over the world have come to Los Angeles. What was once a small pueblo has expanded to become the large and diverse city it is today.

The Ord Survey, drawn in 1849, shows the plan for the city of Los Angeles prior to becoming part of the state of California in 1850.

Los Angeles today.

TIMELINE

1771
Spanish build the San Gabriel Mission.

1781
Mexican settlers colonize and rename Los Angeles.

1856
October 16
Ellen and Charles Owens marry.

11.
HOME

After ten years of working
as a midwife, nurse,
and assistant to Dr. Griffin,
Biddy buys two plots of land
on Spring Street for $250 dollars.
She signs the deed with an X,
but it's printed in her name:
Biddy Mason.

Vineyards spread out
like the sea. A living willow
fence encircles the house.
And orange trees
are so plenty that Biddy,
on this spring afternoon,
reaches up, grabs one,
and puts it in her pocket.

She pulls a few new weeds
from the yerba mansa
and elderberry, giving
them room to flourish.
Now, in her own garden,

Biddy grows the medicinal
plants she needs.

She picks a sprig of mint
and thinks, *If only Ann
could be here, too.*
In her dreams
for her daughters,
Biddy never thought
smallpox would take
Ann from her.

*I wanted you to know
more of this free life, child.*
A breeze lays a gentle
touch on Biddy's heart.

She steps onto the porch
to the laughter of her
grandsons, Robert and Henry.
They chase each other around
until seven-year-old Robert hugs
Biddy's legs. Five-year-old Henry
retreats to Ellen's lap.

Biddys sits with Harriet
and Ellen, and peels
the orange for the boys
to eat. Together, they
watch the pure gold hills
of California poppies.

A carriage drives by,
kicking up dust. Biddy sees
it paint portraits of Granny Ellen

and Ann, and she recalls
the mirage when they walked
across the Mojave Desert.
It was this house, this porch
Granny had been sitting on.

When the dust settles,
Biddy says to her daughters,
"Always retain
your homestead, no matter
your circumstances."

Biddy's seen whole families
migrate to Los Angeles,
toiling in the vineyards,
groves, and flower fields,
but still unable
to earn enough money
to feed themselves
and build a secure life.

Biddy reaches out an open hand
for her daughters to hold.
She says to them,
"Whatever it is you dream,
use this land to grow it."

YERBA MANSA

Yerba mansa can treat swollen gums
and a sore throat.

ESTABLISHING A HOMESTEAD

While Biddy was able to save so many lives, she was devastated when her daughter Ann died at fourteen years old in 1857. In the face of such loss also came new life. Ellen (pictured here in 1863) and Charles had two sons, Robert and Henry. They were born free. Biddy became a grandmother.

Three years after winning her court case, Biddy was hired by Dr. John Strother Griffin, (shown below) to work as a doctor's assistant. In 1859, Dr. Griffin became the official doctor at the county jail and the county hospital, and he needed Biddy's help. She worked for his private practice for $2.50 per day, which is worth about $70 today.

Biddy also continued to run her own midwife and nursing practice. She was known to heal people in the poorer areas of the city, and also people imprisoned in the city jails.

WHAT DOES HOME MEAN TO YOU?

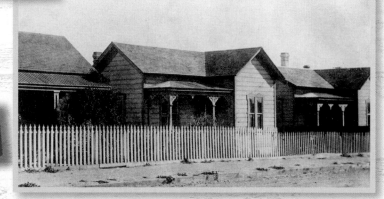

At first, Biddy moved into her own rental home, shown in this photo, which was near the Owens' house on San Pedro Street between First and Second.

Over the next ten years, Biddy carefully saved the money she earned. At forty-eight years old, she was one of the first women to buy land in Los Angeles. For $250 she bought a parcel on Spring Street between Third and Fourth Streets, which at the time was on the outskirts of Los Angeles. The land was described as having "a ditch of water on the place and a willow fence running around the plot of ground." Biddy became the proud owner of her own homestead. She saw this as a legacy for her children and grandchildren.

View of Biddy's Mason's property in 1871, five years after she bought it.

The deed for the property that Biddy bought on Spring Street.

This section of a mural, entitled *History of Medicine in California* and painted by Bernard Zakheim in 1936, shows Biddy and Dr. John Griffin working together.

The Civil War and Reconstruction

The Civil War began in 1861 when the fight between the Northern and Southern states over slavery finally reached a boiling point. Eleven Southern states decided to secede from the United States, forming the Confederacy. The Civil War lasted four long and bloody years until the Confederate Army surrendered in 1865. The Thirteenth Amendment to the United States Constitution abolished slavery across the nation. Freed Black people continued to face severe racism and discrimination, but finally, they legally had their freedom.

SECEDE: to withdraw from being part of an organization, group, or country.

CONFEDERACY: the eleven Southern states that seceded from the United States: Alabama, Arkansas, Tennessee, Mississippi, Florida, Georgia, Texas, North Carolina, South Carolina, Louisiana, and Virginia.

AMENDMENT: a change made to the United States Constitution.

RECRUITMENT: the act of finding new people to sign up for the armed forces.

Free and enslaved Black men were eventually allowed to fight for the North in the Civil War. This recruitment poster was hung in Philadelphia around 1864.

COME AND JOIN US BROTHERS.
PUBLISHED BY THE SUPERVISORY COMMITTEE FOR RECRUITING COLORED REGIMENTS
1210 CHESTNUT ST. PHILADELPHIA.

The Fourteenth Amendment to the Constitution says that anyone born in the United States is a citizen.

TIMELINE

1857
August
Ann dies.

1859
Ellen gives birth to Robert, Biddy's first grandchild.
May
Biddy starts working for Dr. Griffin.

1861
Ellen gives birth to Henry.

1865
The Civil War ends and the Thirteenth Amendment officially abolishes slavery.

After the Civil War, all-White Southern state governments passed codes that stopped Black people from getting work, buying land, and voting. As a response, the United States government added the Fourteenth Amendment to the Constitution, which states that anyone born in the United States is a citizen. This nullifed the Dred Scott decision, and meant that freed enslaved people were officially citizens and had the same rights as other citizens. The Fourteenth Amendment also says that all people have "equal protection of the laws." This means that no matter a person's age, race, or religion, all citizens should be treated the same by the government. This birthright to citizenship and equal protection under the law have become key to our nation's identity, and have been the basis of many court cases in which people have fought for their rights.

The time period after the Civil War from 1865 to 1877 was called Reconstruction. Millions of Black people and poor White people worked together across the Southern states to run for government positions, and to fight for their rights. Around two thousand Black people held public office. In 1870, the Fifteenth Amendment gave Black men the right to vote. But racism continued. Northern states stopped enforcing more equal treatment of Black people in the South, and White supremacists terrorized and killed Black people across the land. White plantation owners and farmers took advantage of formerly enslaved people by hiring them as sharecroppers, trapping them into working hard hours for very little money or opportunity. From the late nineteenth century through the 1960s, state laws known as Jim Crow laws allowed racial segregation to exist legally, and undid many of the advances made by Black people under Reconstruction.

This lithograph shows the first Black members of Congress during Reconstruction.

NULLIFY: to legally cancel or invalidate.

PUBLIC OFFICE: an elected position with the power to carry out a governmental function.

SEGREGATION: the act of keeping people of different racial backgrounds, religions, or genders separate from each other.

1866
November 28
Biddy Mason buys land for $250.

1868
The Fourteenth Amendment gives citizenship to African Americans.

1870
The Fifteenth Amendment gives Black men the right to vote.

1865–1877
Period of Reconstruction.

12.
BUILDING COMMUNITY

On Sunday afternoons, guests drink Biddy's
homemade elderberry wine as they discuss
community news and politics—the presidential election
and Reconstruction, the recent Fourteenth Amendment,
and nationwide fights against discrimination. Biddy's home
is the gathering place for Los Angeles's Black community.

Over the years, a bustling downtown has grown
around Biddy's homestead.
Spring Street now has banks, hotels,
gas street lamps, a fire-engine company,
stage coaches dashing up and down paved roads.

More and more Black migrants are coming
to the city from the North and South.
Families with school-aged children
and pregnant mothers
are growing the community.

One afternoon, Ann Pepper,
Hannah's eldest daughter,
tells about twelve-year-old

Mary Frances Ward in San Francisco,
who's not allowed to attend
an all-White school. A lawyer
was hired to fight for Mary in court.

Biddy says, "It's a shame.
I had to send my grandbabies
five hundred miles away to Oakland.
There they have good schools
that will educate our children."

Winnie Owens suggests
that they hire a lawyer themselves,
and get schools integrated in Los Angeles.

Heads nod, there are "Amens,"
and then a collective "Yes!"
from these women and men born
in states like Biddy's Georgia homeplace.
Now property owners, boardinghouse keepers,
barbers, maids, and teachers—this is Biddy's
pulled-together family. Their passion
and strength spreads like a network
of roots reaching to uplift.

There are times when the line of people
seeking Biddy's care and medicines
wraps around the corner. And Biddy
turns no one away. Granny Ellen's
words continue to ring truth
in her ears: *Nothing good comes
when we close our hands to others.*

Biddy looks around her living room,
sees her guests together in the service
of Black people's physical, political,

and spiritual well-being. She feels
the weight of Granny Ellen's hand
like a feather in her palm, and says,
"We need a church."

The guests begin to discuss
what kind of church, where it will be,
who will be the minister, and time
quickly passes, day turns to dusk.
By meeting's end, the evening air
is sweet with jasmine, and the first
African Methodist Episcopal church
in Los Angeles is officially organized.

Feeling accomplished, everyone raises
their glasses to cheers. Biddy's guests
give a special thanks to her for offering
to pay the church's property taxes and
minister's salary. With an open heart,
Biddy acknowledges everyone
for their contributions and ideas,
because she knows we all grow together
when our hands and hearts are open.

Elderberries are packed with
nutrients, and can improve heart
health and ward off the flu.

ELDERBERRY

"I AM BECAUSE WE ARE"

Los Angeles continued to grow over the years, and in the 1880s Biddy found that her homestead was in the heart of downtown. Historian Delilah Beasley described Biddy's homestead as "the most valuable piece of property in all of beautiful Los Angeles." Biddy was able to sell part of the land for $1,500—six times more than what she had originally paid.

Biddy went on to buy more land, becoming one of the wealthiest people in the city. She deeply believed in helping others, from her family to institutions that served the larger community. She remained an independent single mother, head of her household, and leader in Los Angeles.

UBUNTU: a southern African philosophy that roughly translates to "I AM BECAUSE WE ARE." In this worldview, we actively participate in the well-being of the entire community. An individual is interdependent with others and cannot achieve anything alone.

This is the only known clear photo of Biddy Mason. She was probably in her fifties when it was taken.

Biddy built a two-story brick building on the remaining land, which is visible here under the "Niles Pease Furniture Carpets" sign. She lived upstairs and rented out the downstairs, hosting meetings and creating a gathering place for others in the local Black community.

According to Biddy's great-granddaughter, Gladys Owens Smith (pictured here with her father, Robert, in 1905), Biddy was known to have said: "If you hold your hand closed, nothing good can come in. The open hand is blessed, for it gives in abundance, even as it receives." These words speak to why Biddy became a philanthropist. She used her money and time to help others.

Access to Education

For close to one hundred years, the state of California allowed or required that schools be racially segregated. Parents of children of color often had to organize separate schools if they wanted their children to be educated.

In 1872, African Americans, including members of the Executive Committee of the Colored Convention, brought the case of twelve-year-old Mary Ward, who lived in San Francisco, to the state supreme court. They argued that Black children deserved access to public education because they were United States citizens. The court decided in 1874 that all United States citizens did deserve a public education, and that "separate but equal" schools were acceptable. However, if schools for African American children could not be well maintained, then those children had the right to attend mostly White schools. Many in the Black community felt that this court decision was a victory, though there was still work to do to fully integrate the schools in the state.

This 1890 photo from Spring Street School in Los Angeles shows that there were some integrated classrooms by this time.

In 1872, Biddy was one of the founders of the First African Methodist Episcopal (FAME) Church. They held the first meetings in her home, and she helped to pay the church's taxes and the minister's salary. Biddy also founded and worked in the city's first day nursery for children in Los Angeles, in which caregivers looked after children while their parents, especially their mothers, went to work.

In 1884, major floods in Los Angeles destroyed many homes. Biddy opened an account at a grocery store for people of any background who were displaced. She paid for their food and supplies. Biddy's home at 331 Spring Street became a refuge to many in need. People heard about her generosity and came from far away to ask for her help.

CONGREGATION: a gathering of people.

ACTIVISM: work to change something, whether it's an unfair law or unfair treatment of a person or group.

SOCIAL REFORM: a movement to create gradual changes in institutions so that power is shared more equally among groups of people.

Black Churches

BETHEL AFRICAN METHODIST EPISCOPAL CHURCH, PHILAD.

The First African Methodist Episcopal (FAME) Church, and other Black religious congregations, have played a key role in bringing the Black community together. Churches were, and are, places for spiritual worship, as well as for community support and activism. The Bethel African Methodist Episcopal Church was established in Philadelphia in 1794 (shown here), founded by people of African descent who objected to being segregated in other Methodist churches services because of their ancestry.

People in Black churches organized and raised funds to fight for the rights of their children to get an education, and for other social reform causes. Church members also organized social clubs and other programs, like libraries, book clubs, sports clubs, music concerts, and restaurants.

Today, the FAME Church of Los Angeles is the oldest and one of the largest Black congregations in the city, with more than nineteen thousand members. While the majority of members are Black, the church is open to anyone who wishes to join.

Biddy was known as Grandma Mason within the community. Her grandson Robert Curry Owens, pictured here, called her his "salvation" because she convinced his father to let him follow his dreams of being a politician rather than a farmer or blacksmith. Robert went on to become an important Black leader in Los Angeles. He met influential Black thinkers W. E. B. Du Bois and Booker T. Washington, and donated generously to organizations that worked for the advancement of Black people.

MATERIAL WEALTH: the possessions that we can touch and see that make our lives better.

By 1890, Spring Street between Fourth and Seventh had become the financial center of Los Angeles, a city of over 50,000 people that included 1,258 African Americans. Biddy had a fortune worth $300,000, which would be more than $7.5 million today. She died on January 15, 1891, at the age of seventy-three.

Biddy Mason's legacy reached far beyond her lifetime. Her daughter Ellen and grandsons continued her philanthropic work. The women from the Mason and Owens families were all active members of local clubs that helped young women and people who were sick or poor—people who needed support. Sadly, the family lost much of their material wealth during the Great Depression. But today we can all carry Biddy's words of giving with an open hand, and her spirit of being part of our communities.

HOW CAN YOU TEND TO YOUR COMMUNITY'S WELL-BEING?

Biddy's lasting importance in the city was recognized in this 1909 article from the *Los Angeles Daily Times*, showing Biddy Mason in the top row on the left, and her daughter Ellen in the center of the bottom row.

The FAME Church of Los Angeles created a headstone for Biddy Mason's grave in 1988. Thousands of people attended the ceremony to place it, including Tom Bradley, the first African American mayor of Los Angeles. He declared November 16 to be "Biddy Mason Day" in honor of her legacy.

TIMELINE

1794
The Bethel African Methodist Episcopal Church is founded in Philadelphia.

1868
Biddy buys a second lot on Olive Street for $375.

1872
Biddy holds a meeting that leads to the establishment of the Los Angeles FAME Church.

1874
Ward vs. Flood is decided by the California supreme court.

In 1999, the community came together to create a monument and a Biddy Mason Park on the site of Biddy Mason's original homestead. You can visit the monument in downtown Los Angeles, between Spring Street and Broadway at Third Street. Biddy Mason's descendants attended the unveiling: her great-granddaughter Gladys, her great-great-great-granddaughter Linda, and her great-great-great-great granddaughters Robynn and Cheryl, pictured here.

* * *

1875
Biddy sells half of her Spring Street lot for $1,500.

1884
Biddy sells part of her Olive Street lot for $2,000.
January–May
Flooding displaces people from their homes.

1891
January 15
Biddy dies.

1988
The FAME Church installs Biddy's gravestone.

1999
The Biddy Mason monument is unveiled.

HEALING YOUR COMMUNITY: FROM BIDDY'S DAY TO OURS

HOW CAN YOU BE LIKE BIDDY AND EXTEND AN OPEN HEART AND HAND TO YOUR COMMUNITY?

When you look around your school and community, do you see people being treated unfairly? When you watch the news or read articles online, do you recognize that some groups of people are experiencing more violence, or are denied basic human rights? And when you look into your heart, how does this make you feel?

Although Biddy cared for and helped all members of her community, she was emotionally invested in the well-being of the Black community. When Biddy spoke up for her freedom, she spoke up for the humanity of all Black people. She intimately understood the particular struggles faced by Black people during her times, and her shared empathy allowed her to be of better service to others. She was able to relate, and that strengthened her relationships.

What social justice issues do you have a personal or emotional connection to? What makes you feel unsafe because of the body you are in? What and who needs love? When we feel personally connected to injustice, we are often more moved to change it.

These organizations were started by women who could no longer be silent regarding the dehumanization of Black life:

Black Lives Matter was founded by three Black and queer women to bring attention to institutional and police violence against Black lives. It is now made up of more than forty member-led chapters around the globe. www.blacklivesmatter.com

Black Women for Wellness was started by a group of women in Los Angeles, and supports the well-being and health of Black women and girls through health education, empowerment, and advocacy. www.bwwla.org

REGINA EVANS, MODERN-DAY ABOLITIONIST

Like Biddy Mason, Regina Evans was enslaved, and her experiences moved her to become an abolitionist. Today slavery looks and operates much differently than it did during Biddy's time, when it was legal. Modern slavery is illegal, and thus more secretive and hidden. People are forced, tricked into, or threatened to provide labor or sex acts against their will. This is known as human trafficking, and it is a multibillion-dollar industry, denying more than twenty million people their freedom. Human trafficking happens in the United States and worldwide. Current research shows that one in seven reported runaway children in the United States were victims of child sex trafficking. For the production of sugarcane, forced child labor throughout the world is used to sweeten our treats.

Regina Evans is a survivor of sex trafficking. She is a poet, playwright, performer, and a trained modern-day abolitionist. She opened Regina's Door in 2014, a healing and sanctuary space in Oakland, California, for young artists and survivors of sex trafficking. Regina sells boutique vintage clothing to fund theater shows, spoken-word events, music concerts, and workshops in dance, arts and crafts, and creative writing. Regina says she wanted "to build a space where survivors could come and rest, feel the flow of love, and manifest, through the arts, the beauty which resides within their beings."

As an entrepreneur and healing artist, Regina Evans continues Biddy Mason's legacy by giving back to her community. Like Biddy, she is also a philanthropist, using money from the boutique to help support Seek and Save, a ministry in Oakland that helps underserved youth, including those who have been trafficked. Regina believes that "Life begins as we extend our hearts, hands, and resources to those who are in need of care and compassion." Visit www.reginasdoor.com to learn more.

Regina reminds us that trafficking is "one of those beasts that is often hidden in plain sight." Learn the warning signs. Get informed and research ways you can help. These organizations provide ways to get involved:

Polaris Project takes action by writing to senators and signing petitions to urge Congress to fight human trafficking online.
www.polarisproject.org

No Traffick Ahead works to educate and raise awareness about the reality that people in our communities are victims of human trafficking.
www.notraffickahead.com

Shared Hope International offers training, resources, and programs to help community members identify signs of trafficking and use their skills to intervene on behalf of child-trafficked victims.
www.sharedhope.org

ACKNOWLEDGMENTS

We are deeply grateful to the many people who assisted us with this book. The ACLU of Northern California, and in particular Executive Director Abdi Soltani as well as Candice Francis and Kendra Fox-Davis, have been major supporters of this book and the series. Several educators, librarians, scholars, and writers helped us to shape the content of this book and offered helpful feedback on drafts: Susan Anderson, Ann Berlak, Jennifer Brouhard, Gardenia Campos, Zetta Elliott, Elaine Elinson, DeEtta Demeratus, Rachel Reinhard, and Blake Norton of the Citizen Potawatomi Nation Cultural Heritage Center. Especially big appreciation goes to scholar Ebony Thomas for connecting us to scholar Sherea Mosley, whose expert guidance on creating a book for middle-grade readers about slavery was invaluable. This book would not be the same without her. And finally, massive appreciation to Stan Yogi, for his vision in cowriting the first book in this series, and for his help in conceiving the series as a whole.

The stellar team at Heyday was critical to the creation of this book. Publisher Steve Wasserman has continued to support and champion Malcolm Margolin's idea for a series of children's books about civil liberties changemakers. Editorial Director Gayle Wattawa provided useful suggestions and asked rigorous questions throughout the process. Illustrator Laura Freeman vibrantly portrayed Biddy Mason's nature-based and spiritual life, while designer Nancy Austin and art director Diane Lee visually brought it together. Terria Smith helped to assess the content about Native Californians. Editor Molly Woodward, on this journey from beginning to end, encouraged us forward and gave us thoughtful feedback. She went far and beyond the expectations for an editor, and we share with her our deepest gratitude.

Laura would like to thank her family and Mitch for all of their support, and especially her daughter, Cassy, and her mother, Carol. Their love and activism inspire her to speak up for justice.

Arisa thanks her wife, Samantha Florio, for her patience; Aunt Bernice Biggs for reminding her that her great-great-grandmother was a midwife; and Aya de Leon for recommending her for this project.

In writing a book like this, we had to make choices about which details to include and which to leave out. We selected details that felt most important in telling Biddy's story in the most accurate and compelling way—but writing nonfiction always means finding our own version of the story. Any inaccuracies are our own.

❋ ❋ ❋

Heyday thanks the following donors for their generous contributions to this project:

Karen and Thomas Mulvaney

Suzanne Abel; Carrie Avery and Jon Tigar; Judy Avery; Lucinda Barnes; Jennifer Bates; Richard and Rickie Ann Baum; Sara Becker;

Kate Black; Barbara Boucke; Barbara and John Boyle; John Briscoe; David and Pamela Bullen; Helen Cagampang; Bea Calo; Joanne Campbell; Dennis Carty; James and Margaret Chapin; David Chu; Cynthia Clarke; Raymond and Eva Cook; Roberta Cordero; Steve Costa and Kate Levinson; Robert Dawson and Ellen Manchester; Thomas Delebo and Bernie Feeney; Chris Desser and Kirk Marckwald; Lokelani Devone and Annette Brand; Michael Eaton and Charity Kenyon; Judith and Robert Flynn; Patrick Golden; Elizabeth Goldstein; Dr. Erica and Barry Goode; James Guerard; Kenji Hakuta and Nancy Goodban; Cricket Halsey; Francine Hartman and Chris De Marco; Anna Hawken; Nettie Hoge; Donna Ewald Huggins; Tom Killion; Susan Kirsch; Guy Lampard and Suzanne Badenhoop; Rebecca LeGates and Jonathan Root; Kerry and Dewey Livingston; David Loeb; Gary Malazian; Reuben Margolin and Amber Menzies; Kathy Martinez; Pamela Mendelsohn; Mary and Joe Morganti; Mark Murphy; Richard Nagler; Jean and Gary Pokorny; James and Caren Quay; Steven Rasmussen and Felicia Woytak; Kristine Reveles; Robin Ridder; Lennie and Mike Roberts; Alexandra Rome; Spreck Rosekrans and Isabella Salaverry; Peter Rosenwald; Becky Saeger and Tom Graves; Joanne Sakai and Dallas Foster; Peter Schrag and Patricia Ternahan Ttee; Toby and Sheila Schwartzburg; Mary Selkirk and Lee Ballance; Peter Selz and Carole Schemmerling; Jennifer Sime; Carla Soracco and Donna Fong; Linda Spencer; Kimberly Stevenot; Azile and Marcus White; and Al Young.

SOURCE NOTES

Beyond the primary texts listed in the bibliography, these texts informed particular chapters.

INTRODUCTION

"Nothing good...hand": Sue Bailey Thurman, *Pioneers of Negro Origin in California*, 47 (see bibliography).

1. HEALING

Pages 1 and 2, stanzas 2 and 5: Sarah Mitchell, "The Transfer of Slave Medical Knowledge," *Bodies of Knowledge: The Influence of Slaves on the Antebellum Medical Community* (Doctoral dissertation), 1997, hdl.handle.net/10919/36885.

Page 2, stanza 7: William Francis, Charles Pickard Ware, and Lucy McKim Garrison, "I'm Going Home," *Slave Songs of the United States: Electronic Edition*, http://docsouth.unc.edu/church/allen/allen.html.

Pages 2–3: stanza 9: Maisah B. Robinson, Ph.D, and Frank H. Robinson Sr., MD, "Slave Medicine: Herbal Lessons from American History," http://www.motherearthliving.com.

Page 4: stanza 15: Glenda Sullivan, "Plantation Medicine and Health Care in the Old South," *Legacy* 10, no. 1 (2010): article 3.

Pages 5–6: Teaching Hard History from Teaching Tolerance influenced the section on slavery with its Key Concept 4: "'Slavery was an institution of power,' designed to create profit for the enslavers and break the will of the enslaved and was a relentless quest for profit abetted by racism"; and Key Concept 8: "Slavery shaped the fundamental beliefs of Americans about race and whiteness, and white supremacy was both a product and legacy of slavery." The section on the US Constitution was influenced by Key Concept 3: "Protections for slavery were embedded in the founding documents; enslavers dominated the federal government, Supreme Court and Senate from 1787 through 1860."

Page 6: The "Power Discussed" section was based on Maurianne Adams, Lee Anne Bell, and Pat Griffin, Eds. *Teaching for Diversity and Social Justice: Second Edition* (New York: Routledge, 2007), 190.

Page 6: The section on midwives was influenced by Barbara Hathaway, *Missy Violet and Me* (New York:

HMH Books for Young Readers, 2008) and Jacqueline Jones, *Labor of Love, Labor of Sorrow: Black Women, Work, and the Family, From Slavery to the Present* (New York: Vintage Books,1986), 40–41.

2. PLANTATION WOUNDS

Pages 12–13: Key books that influenced this section were Belinda Hurmence's *Slavery Time When I Was Chillun* (New York: G.P. Putnam's and Sons, 1997) and Julius Lester's *To Be a Slave* (New York: Dial, 1968).

Page 12: "The crack of...bedtime": Solomon Northup, *Twelve Years a Slave: Narrative of Solomon Northup, a Citizen of New-York, Kidnapped in Washington City in 1841, and Rescued in 1853* (Chapel Hill, University of North Carolina at Chapel Hill, 1997), 179; electronic edition: http://docsouth.unc.edu/fpn/northup/northup.html.

Page 13: "Any person...lashes": William W. Brown, Narrative of William W. Brown, a Fugitive Slave (Boston: Anti-Slavery Office, 1848), 134–135; electronic edition: http://docsouth.unc.edu/neh/brown47/menu.html.

Page 13: Slave Codes: Philadelphia Female Anti-Slavery Society, "Extracts from the American Slave Codes," internet archive, https://archive.org/details/extractsfromamer00phil.

Page 13; "[w]ashing dishes...cotton": *Federal Writers' Project: Slave Narrative Project, Vol. 2, Arkansas, Part 3, Gadson-Isom,* 1936, courtesy of the Library of Congress, https://www.loc.gov/item/mesn023.

Page 13: "I weren't...wood": *Federal Writers' Project: Slave Narrative Project, Vol. 1, Alabama, Aarons-Young, 1936,* https://www.loc.gov/item/mesn010/.

3. STOLEN AND CARRIED AWAY

Page 18: A key book that influenced this section was Wilma King's *Stolen Childhood*, 46–50 and 212–261 (see bibliography).

Page 20: Teaching Hard History from Teaching Tolerance influenced the section on the economy of slavery with its Key Concept 2: "Slavery and the slave trade were central to the development and growth of the economy across British North America and, later, the United States."

Page 21: Harriet Ann Jacobs's *Incidents in the Life of a*

Slave Girl Written by Herself, published in 1861 (http://docsouth.unc.edu/fpn/jacobs/jacobs.html), was formative for us in looking at being an enslaved girl and woman and facing sexual violence.

4. LONG WALK WEST, 1848

Page 25, stanzas 12–13 about Potawatomi plant medicines: courtesy of the Citizen Potawatomi Nation Cultural Heritage Center.

Page 26, stanzas 16–20: King, "In the Beginning": The Transatlantic Trade in Children of African Descent," in *Stolen Childhood,* 1–29.

Page 29: The Trans-Atlantic Slave Trade and Middle Passage section was informed by the Slave Voyages website, http://www.slavevoyages.org. Other sources for this section include: "Mormonism in Pictures: Pioneers' Trek West," https://www.mormonnewsroom.org/article/mormonism-pictures-pioneers-trek-west; and the National Oregon/California Trail Center at Montpelier, Idaho.

5. COTTONWOOD, UTAH

Page 32, stanza 9: Robinson and Robinson, "Slave Medicine: Herbal Lessons from American History."

Page 34: Quintard Taylor's *In Search of the Racial Frontier: African Americans in the American West, 1528-1990* (New York: Norton, 1998) was especially informative about the Black community in Utah.

Page 34: In her 1850 diary, a White Mormon woman named Eliza Lyman describes how Jane James gave her supplies when her husband, Amasa, was away: "Not long after Amasa had gone, Jane James, the colored woman, let me have two pounds of flour, it being half of what she had." This inspired the scene we created. From Henry J. Wolfinger, "A Test of Faith: Jane Elizabeth Manning James and the Origins of the Utah Black Community" (1893), series MSS SC 1069, pages 3–2, Tom Perry Special Collections, Harold B. Lee Library, Brigham Young University.

6. CALIFORNIA DREAMING

Page 38, stanza 5: *Bridget "Biddy" Mason: From Slave to Businesswoman,* 48–49 (see bibliography).

Page 38: stanza 9, and page 40: Allen, Ware, and Garrison, "I'm Going Home." We also drew on the Library of Congress's African American Song resource, which includes more on songs during slavery: https://www.loc.gov/item/ihas.200197451.

Page 40: The information on Lizzy Flake Rowan is in part from the City of San Bernardino website, https://www.ci-san bernardino.ca.us/about/history/lizzy_flake_rowan___slave.asp.

Page 41: This map, which can be enlarged online, shows free states, slave states, and undetermined territories as of 1850: https://digital.lib.uh.edu/collection/p15195coll35/item/28.

7. FREEDOM FOR SOME

Page 44, stanza 9: DeEtta Demaratus, "The Writ," *The Force of a Feather,* 78–80 (see bibliography).

Page 45, stanza 13: Demaratus, "The Verdict," *The Force of a Feather,* 111.

Page 47: In her interview with author Delilah Beasley for her book *The Negro Trail Blazers of California* (see bibliography), Biddy's daughter Ellen reported that Lizzy Rowan passed on the news that Biddy and the others were being taken to Texas (page 90). Dolores Hayden in *The Power of Place* (see bibliography) lists both Lizzy Rowan and Charles Owens.

Page 48: Elaine Elinson and Stan Yogi's *Wherever There's a Fight: How Runaway Slaves, Suffragists, Immigrants, Strikers, and Poets Shaped Civil Liberties in California* (Berkeley: Heyday, 2009) was a key source about California and the law (12–14) and the enslavement of Native Californians (18). Information on the Owens family comes from *The Negro Trail Blazers of California* (110) and "My Grandfather" and "Autobiography" written by Robert Owens (son of Charles), held at Golden State Mutual Life Insurance Company records (Collection 1434), Library Special Collections, Charles E. Young Research Library, UCLA.

8. HOPE

Page 54: "The coldest...experienced": Demeratus, *The Force of a Feather*, 50.

Page 54: The full list of people who may have reported to the sheriff, including members of the Colored Convention, in Demaratus, *The Force of a Feather*, 223.

Page 55: The section on resistance, especially the emphasis on everyday acts of resistance, was influenced by Teaching Hard History Key Concept 5: "Enslaved people resisted the efforts of their enslavers to reduce them to commodities in both revolutionary and everyday ways."

9. VERDICT, 1856

Page 59: "I have...to do" and "I always...of it": Hayden, *The Power of Place,* 149.

Page 60: "I do not...to go": Demaratus, *The Force of a Feather,* 111;

Page 60: "are free forever": *Mason v. Smith* decision from 1856, University of California, Los Angeles, Department of Special Collections, Charles E. Young Research Library.

Pages 60–61: The verdict is found in the Golden States Insurance Company Records, and the full text can be viewed at BlackPast.org: http://www.blackpast.org/primarywest/mason-v-smith-bridget-biddy-mason-case-1856.

Page 61: "left Mississippi...as slaves": Demaratus, *The Force of a Feather*, 83.

Page 61: "I do not...go": Demaratus, *The Force of a Feather*, 111.

Page 63: The section on Colored Conventions was informed by the website Colored Conventions: Bringing Nineteenth-Century Black Organizing to Digital Life, http://www.coloredconventions.org.

10. LIVING FREE

Page 65, stanza 2: Demaratus, "Five Codas," *The Force of a Feather*, 172–173.

Page 68: "become settled...without fear": Hayden, *The Power of Place*, 151.

Page 69: Information in "The Mason, Owens, and Embers Families: A Growing Network" was drawn from Marne L. Campbell, *Making Black Los Angeles* (Chapel Hill: University of North Carolina Press, 2016), chapter two.

Page 69: "Whatever...things": Camille Gavin, *A Place of Her Own* (Baltimore: Publish America, 2007), 37.

Page 69: "Table: Race in Los Angeles" was drawn from Campbell, *Making Black Los Angeles,* chapter one.

11. HOME

Page 73, stanza 2: Hayden, *The Power of Place,* 160.

Page 75, stanza 9: Beasley, *The Negro Trail Blazers of California*, 90.

Page 76: "a ditch of water...plot of ground": Beasley, *The Negro Trail Blazers of California,* 109.

Page 77: This map showing Biddy Mason's property allows viewers to zoom in and out, giving an excellent overview of this part of Los Angeles in 1871: http://imgzoom.cdlib.org/Fullscreen.ics?ark=ark:/13030/hb467nb63s/z1&&brand=oac4.

Pages 78–79: The section on Reconstruction was informed by educational material developed by the Zinn Education Project, https://zinnedproject.org/about/teach-reconstruction.

12. BUILDING COMMUNITY

Pages 81–82, stanza 4, and page 85, "Access to Education": Elaine Elinson and Stan Yogi, "Under Color of Law," *Wherever There's A Fight,* 130.

Page 82, stanza 5: Beasley, *The Negro Trail Blazers of California,* 109–110.

Page 84: Ubuntu, "I am because we are": Cynthia B. Dillard, *Learning to (Re)member the Things We've Learned to Forget,* 83–105 (see bibliography).

Page 84: "the most...Los Angeles": Beasley, *The Negro Trail Blazers of California,* 109.

Page 84: "If you hold...as it receives": Sue Bailey Thurman, *Pioneers of Negro Origin in California,* 47 (see bibliography).

Page 85: Information about Robert Owens and his children was found in the article "Robert C. Owens: A Pacific Coast Successful Negro," from *Colored American Magazine*. The article, and the entire magazine, are available online: https://babel.hathitrust.org/cgi/pt?id=uc1.b3793665;view=1up;seq=421.

BIBLIOGRAPHY

BOOKS

Key Texts That Provided Information about Biddy Mason

Bailey Thurman, Sue. *Pioneers of Negro Origin in California.* San Francisco: Acme, 1952. Contains a section on Biddy Mason based on an interview with her great-granddaughter Gladys, the source of the "open hand" quote.

Beasley, Delilah L. *The Negro Trail Blazers of California.* Los Angeles: Bancroft Library, 1919. A key source text about Black California history in general, with two sections about Biddy Mason based in part on an interview with her daughter Ellen. Full text available online at https://archive.org/details/negrotrailblazer 00beas.

Campbell, Marne L. *Making Black Los Angeles: Class, Gender, and Community, 1850–1917.* Chapel Hill: University of North Carolina Press, 2016. Provides extensive research on original Black individuals and community in Los Angeles, including Biddy Mason.

Demaratus, DeEtta. *The Force of a Feather: The Search for a Lost Story of Slavery and Freedom.* Salt Lake City: University of Utah Press, 2002. Useful for extensive primary source research, especially on the Smiths, and on Biddy Mason's westward journey and the trial.

Hayden, Dolores. *The Power of Place: Urban Landscapes as Public History.* Cambridge, MA: MIT Press, 1995. Key for information on Biddy's life in Los Angeles and the creation of the monument in her honor.

Ruddick, Susan M. and Mary-Beth Welch. *The Story of Biddy Mason.* Paper submitted for Dolores Hayden's course titled Los Angeles Place Making. UCLA Graduate School of Architecture and Urban Planning, February 1984, http://www.publicartinla.com/Downtown /Broadway/Biddy_Mason/ruddick_Biddy_Mason.htm. Excellent information about changes in Los Angeles during Biddy Mason's time.

Other Key Informative Texts

Adams, Maurianne, Lee Anne Bell, and Pat Griffin, Eds. *Teaching for Diversity and Social Justice: Second Edition.* New York: Routledge, 2007.

Dillard, Cynthia B. *Learning to (Re)member the Things We've Learned to Forget: Endarkened Feminisms, Spirituality, and the Sacred Nature of Research and Teaching.* New York: Peter Lang Publishing, Inc., 2012.

Jones, Jacqueline. *Labor of Love, Labor of Sorrow: Black Women, Work, and the Family, From Slavery to the Present.* New York: Vintage Books, 1986.

King, Wilma. *Stolen Childhood: Slave Youth in Nineteenth-Century America.* Second Edition. Bloomington: Indiana University Press, 2011.

Books for Young Readers about Biddy Mason that Influenced Ours

Gavin, Camille. *Biddy Mason: A Place of Her Own.* Baltimore: Publish America, 2007.

Robinson, Deidre. *Open Hands, Open Heart: The Story of Biddy Mason.* Illustrated by Albert T. Cooper III. Gardena, CA: Sly Fox Publishing Company, 1998.

Williams, Jean Kinney. *Bridget "Biddy" Mason: From Slave to Businesswoman.* Minneapolis: Compass Point Books, 2006.

ONLINE RESOURCES

Documenting the American South: A digital publishing initiative that provides Internet access to texts, images, and audio files related to Southern history, literature, and culture, including a vast collection of complete "Slave Narratives." www.docsouth.unc.edu.

Teaching for Change and the Zinn Education Project: Providing books, lesson plans, and educators' resources for teaching social justice in the classroom. www.teachingforchange.org.

Teaching Hard History: A study and teaching resources from Teaching Tolerance of the Southern Poverty Law Center, showing how slavery has been inadequately taught in classrooms and providing a framework for teaching US slavery. www.splcenter.org/teaching -hard-history-american-slavery.

The Trans-Atlantic Slave Trade Database: Information on nearly 36,000 slaving voyages that forcibly transported over 10 million Africans to the Americas between the sixteenth and nineteenth centuries. www.slavevoyages.org.

Voices from the Days of Slavery: Former Slaves Tell Their Stories: From the Library of Congress, an archive of recorded interviews that took place between 1932 and 1975. www.memory.loc.gov /ammem/collections/voices.

IMAGE CREDITS AND PERMISSIONS

Heyday thanks the museums, public agencies, and private collections from which the images in this book were borrowed. Simon Elliott at UCLA was especially helpful, for which we are grateful.

1. HEALING

Page 3: photo by Larry Rana, US Department of Agriculture, August 1995, https://www.flickr.com/photos/usdagov

Page 4: photo by Pedrik, September 9, 2017, https://www.flickr.com/photos/pedrik

Page 5: "Slave auction bill," courtesy of Schomburg Center for Research in Black Culture, Manuscripts, Archives, and Rare Books Division, The New York Public Library, New York Public Library Digital Collections; bottom: courtesy of the National Archives and Records Administration

Page 6: photo by Timothy H. O'Sullivan, 1862, courtesy of the National Archives and Records Administration (cwp2003004651/PP)

Page 7: top: photo by Orin Sage Wightman from *Early Days in Coastal Georgia,* written by Margaret Davis Cate, Fort Frederica Association, 1955; bottom: "The broomstick wedding," courtesy of Schomburg Center for Research in Black Culture, Jean Blackwell Hutson Research and Reference Division, The New York Public Library, New York Public Library Digital Collections

2. PLANTATION WOUNDS

Page 11: photo by H. Zell, June 27, 2009, https://commons.wikimedia.org/wiki/File:Plantago_major_002.JPG

Page 12: top: photo by Mathew Brady, c. 1862, courtesy of the National Archives and Records Administration (2010647787); bottom: photo by Pierre Havens, 1850s, courtesy of New York Historical Society

Page 13: left: photo by J. H. Aylsworth, 1860s, Collection of the Smithsonian National Museum of African American History and Culture (2008.9.26); right: photo by Jay Phagan, May 28, 2010, https://www.flickr.com/photos/jayphagan/6583128607.

3. STOLEN AND CARRIED AWAY

Page 17: photo by Kirstine Paulus, May 25, 2014, https://www.flickr.com/photos/kpaulus/14081647007

Page 18: top: courtesy of the Rare Book and Special Collections Division, the Library of Congress, Washington, DC (2002698281); bottom: Ashley's Sack, Charleston, South Carolina, courtesy of the Middleton Place Foundation

Page 19: top: photo of Rebecca Smith from *South Carolina to Texas (the Long Way),* compiled and edited by Bob Weed and Ethel Klemcke, 1988, used courtesy of Michael Moyette; middle: photo by Dorothea Lange, July 1937, courtesy of the National Archives and Records Administration (2017770305)

Page 20: top: Ellis, Leonard B., O.H. Bailey & Co, and C.H. Vogt (Firm), "View of the city of New Bedford, Mass," Map, 1876, Norman B. Leventhal Map Center, https://collections.leventhalmap.org/search/commonwealth:x633fc62k; center: 1862 100 dollar bill sourced from planetoddity.com; bottom: photo by Ad Meskens, July 2007, https://commons.wikimedia.org/wiki/File:White_House_02.jpg

Page 21: left: photo by M. H. Kimball, c. 1863, courtesy of the National Archives and Records Administration (2010647842); right: Harriet Powers's quilt, 1895–1898, bequest of Maxim Karolik, courtesy of Museum of Fine Arts Boston (description of images depicted in panels here: http://www.mfa.org/collections/object/pictorial-quilt-116166), photograph © 2019 Museum of Fine Arts, Boston

4. LONG WALK WEST, 1848

Page 26: photo by H. Zell, 20 June 2010, https://commons.wikimedia.org/wiki/File:Calla_palustris_2.JPG

Page 28: top: drawing of Potawatomi woman from the 1830s courtesy of Citizen Potawatomi Nation Cultural Heritage Center; middle: *Winter Quarters* by C. C. A. Christensen (1831–1912), c. 1878, tempera on muslin, 76 3/4 x 113 3/4 inches, Brigham Young University Museum of Art, gift of the grandchildren of C.C.A. Christensen, 1970.

Page 29: bottom: "Stowage of the British slave ship Brookes under the regulated slave trade act of 1788," courtesy of the Library of Congress Rare Book and Special Collections Division (USZ62-44000)

5. COTTONWOOD, UTAH

Page 33: photo of mustard sourced from Pixnio

Page 34: top: *The Great Salt Lake* by Thomas Moran, courtesy of the Boston Public Library (07_11_000200); middle: "An Extemporized Dolly Varden," *Harpers Weekly,* July 13, 1872, as drawn by W. L. Sheppard; bottom: photo of Jane Elizabeth Manning James, photographer unknown, https://commons.wikimedia.org/wiki/File:Jane_Elizabeth_Manning_James.jpg

Page 35: right: 1828 Manumission note, https://commons.wikimedia.org/wiki/File:1828_Manumission_Note.jpg

6. CALIFORNIA DREAMING

Page 39: photo by Mark Gunn, June 6, 2016, https://www.flickr.com/photos/mark-gunn/27410913851

Page 40: middle left: "Plantation slave singers; All clapped hand in unison, until the air quivered with melody," Schomburg Center for Research in Black Culture, Jean Blackwell Hutson Research and Reference Division, The New York Public Library, New York Public Library Digital Collections; middle right: musical notation for "I'm Going Home," in *Slave Songs of the United States,* by William Francis Allen, New York: A. Simpson and Co., 1867, http://docsouth.unc.edu/church/allen/fig130.html; bottom: photo courtesy of Alice Johnson Black, http://sbcity.org/about/history/pioneer_women/alice_rowan_johnson.asp

Page 41: top: United States, approximately 1856, Historic Maps, Special Collections, University of Houston Libraries, http://digital.lib.uh.edu/collection/p15195coll35/item/28; bottom: Effects of the Fugitive-Slave-Law, courtesy of the National Archives and Records Administration (2008661523)

7. FREEDOM FOR SOME

Page 46: photo by Sheila Brown, http://www.publicdomainpictures.net/view-image.php?image=237344&picture=juniper-berries-close-up

Page 47: top: N. Orr, engraving of Mormon settlement in San Bernardino, courtesy of the Bancroft Library (BANC PIC 1963.002:0479:02—A); bottom: photo of store on Main and Commercial Streets, 1870, Security Pacific National Bank Collection, Los Angeles Public Library (00068500)

Page 48: top: Records of the Constitutional Convention of 1849, California State Archives, Secretary of State of California; middle: photo of Maidu boy by Robert H. Vance, c. 1850, collection SFMOMA, purchased through a gift of Lucinda Watson, the Evelyn and Walter Haas, Jr. Fund, an anonymous gift, H. Marcia Smolens, Tony and I'lee Hooker, and the Accessions Committee Fund

Page 49: middle left: Los Angeles, Los Angeles County, Cal. 1857 by Britton, Rey, and Co. University of California, Los Angeles, Library, Henry J. Bruman Map Collection; middle right: photo by Erwin H. Smith of African American cowboys on their mounts ready to participate in a horse race during Negro State Fair, Bonham, Texas, c. 1911–1915 (LC-S611-016), courtesy of the Erwin E. Smith Collection of the Library of Congress on deposit at the Amon Carter Museum of American Art, Fort Worth, Texas, © Erwin E. Smith Foundation

8. HOPE

Page 54: top: photo by National Park Service, https://www.nationalparks.org/sites/default/files/styles/wide_1x/public/SantaMonica_image%202.jpg?itok=-jfZQMx9; bottom: courtesy of the National Archives and Records Administration

Page 55: middle: *Nat Turner Urging the Slaves to Rebellion* by Lorenzo Harris, sourced from Revisiting Rebellion: Nat Turner in the American Imagination, http://americanantiquarian.org/NatTurner/items/show/48; bottom: courtesy of the National Archives and Records Administration (SZ62-7816)

9. VERDICT, 1856

Page 60: photo by Jason Hollinger, March 11, 2005, https://commons.wikimedia.org/wiki/File:California_Poppy_-_Flickr_-_pellaea.jpg

Page 61: top: University of Southern California, Libraries and California Historical Society (CHS-1860); bottom: University of Southern California, Libraries and California Historical Society (CHS-11939)

Page 62: oil on canvas portrait of Dred Scott by Louis Schultze, ca. 1890, courtesy of the Missouri Historical Society (1897-009-0001)

Page 63: left: Proceedings of the first State Convention of the Colored Citizens of the State of California, Samuel J. May Anti-Slavery Collection, the Division of Rare and Manuscript Collections, Cornell University

Library; right: illustration of the National Colored Convention in Washington, DC, published in *Harper's Weekly,* February 6, 1869, page 65

10. LIVING FREE

Page 67: photo of White Sage sourced from Max Pixel

Page 68: middle: Golden State Mutual Life Insurance Company records (Collection 1434), Library Special Collections, Charles E. Young Research Library, UCLA; bottom: photo by Laura Atkins from Biddy Mason monument; original freedom papers, Golden State Mutual Life Insurance Company records (Collection 1434), Library Special Collections, Charles E. Young Research Library, UCLA

Page 70: middle: photo of Tongva Nation Dancers at the Moompetam Native American Festival at the Aquarium of the Pacific in Long Beach, CA, by Kayte Deioma, 2013; bottom: photo of Pío Pico courtesy of University of Southern California, Libraries and California Historical Society (isla id: 1-90-510)

Page 71: top: courtesy of University of Southern California, Libraries and California Historical Society (CHS-6040); bottom: photo by Navid Serrano, Dec. 10, 2007, https://commons.wikimedia.org/wiki/File :LA_Skyline_Mountains2.jpg

11. HOME

Page 75: photo by Stickpen, May 13, 2009, https://com mons.wikimedia.org/wiki/File:Anemopsis.jpg

Page 76: top right and bottom: photos of Ellen and Biddy's first rental home, Golden State Mutual Life Insurance Company records (Collection 1434), Library Special Collections, Charles E. Young Research Library, UCLA; middle: Los Angeles Public Library, Security Pacific National Bank Collection

Page 77: middle: City of Los Angeles, drawn by August Koch, 1871, courtesy of UCLA Special Collections, Charles E. Young Research Library; bottom left: Bernard Zakheim mural image, MSS 2014-15, UCSF Library, Archives and Special Collections, University of California, San Francisco; bottom right: Golden State Mutual Life Insurance Company records (Collection 1434), Library Special Collections, Charles E. Young Research Library, UCLA

Page 78: middle: Come and Join Us Brothers, US Colored Troop Recruitment broadside, 1863–1865, Rare Book, Manuscript, and Special Collections Library at Duke University; bottom: courtesy of the National Archives and Records Administration

Page 79: courtesy of the National Archives and Records Administration (98501907)

12. BUILDING COMMUNITY

Page 83: photo by Edal Anton Lefterov, August 19, 2007, https://commons.wikimedia.org/wiki/File:Sam bucus-berries.jpg

Page 84: top: Golden State Mutual Life Insurance Company records (Collection 1434), Library Special Collections, Charles E. Young Research Library, UCLA; bottom: UCLA Library Special Collections

Page 85: top: The *Colored American Magazine* 8–9, 1905, https://babel.hathitrust.org/cgi/pt?id=uc1. b3793665;view=1up;seq=421; bottom: photo of Spring Street School students by J. B. Blanchard, 1890, Security Pacific National Bank Collection, Los Angeles Public Library

Page 86: middle: Bethel AME Church, 1829, sourced from http://www.blackpast.org; bottom: photo by Laurie Avocado, July 1, 2009, https://commons.wiki media.org/wiki/File:First_AME_Church_Los_Angeles .jpg

Page 87: top: photo of Robert Owens, sourced from http://www.blackpast.org; bottom: "The Negro Woman in Los Angeles and Vicinity—Some Notable Characters," by Kate Bradley Stovall, *Los Angeles Daily Times*, Friday, February 12, 1909, http://latimes blogs.latimes.com/thedailymirror/files/1909_0212 _black_women.jpg

Page 88: photo of Biddy Mason's grave by Jim Lovelace

Page 89: photo by Dolores Hayden, *The Power of Place: Urban Landscapes as Public History*, figure 7.9, © 1995 Massachusetts Institute of Technology, with permission of the MIT Press

INDEX

ABOUT THE AUTHORS

photo: Nye' Lyn Tho

photo: Jan Thyer

Arisa White is a poet and educator whose work was nominated for a Lambda Literary Award and NAACP Image Award. Her recent poetry collection is *You're the Most Beautiful Thing That Happened.* To read more about her writing, visit arisawhite.com.

Laura Atkins is a children's book author and editor who grew up in an activist family and participates in social justice work herself, with a focus on diversity and equity in children's books. She lives in Berkeley, California, with her daughter and their dog. Find out more at lauraatkins.com.

ABOUT THE ILLUSTRATOR

photo: Milo Hines

Laura Freeman is an Illustrator of children's books, editorial content, and licensed art. She's also a mom, a gardener, and a Photoshop junkie. She's a displaced New Yorker, currently living in Atlanta, Georgia, with her husband and two children. To see more of her work, visit LFreemanArt.com.